THE GLORY YEARS

Old-Time
BASEBALL
TRIVIA

KERRY BANKS

GREYSTONE BOOKS

DOUGLAS & MCINTYRE

VANCOUVER/TORONTO

For the home team: Anne and Riley

Greystone Books
A division of Douglas & McIntyre Ltd.
1615 Venables Street
Vancouver, British Columbia V5L 2H1

Canadian Cataloguing in Publication Data
Banks, Kerry, 1952 –
    Old-time baseball trivia

    ISBN 1-55054-531-0

    1. Baseball—Miscellanea. I. Title
GV867.3.B36 1997   796.357   C97-910004-6

Editing by Brian Scrivener
Cover and text design by Peter Cocking
Front cover photograph courtesy National Baseball Hall of Fame Library,
    Cooperstown N.Y./Carl Seid
Back cover photograph courtesy UPI/Corbis-Bettmann
Printed and bound in Canada by Best Book Manufacturers

Every reasonable care has been taken to trace the ownership of copyrighted visual material. Information that will enable the publisher to rectify any reference or credit is welcome.

The publisher gratefully acknowledges the assistance of the Canada Council and of the British Columbia Ministry of Tourism, Small Business and Culture.

Contents

PREFACE

The transistor radio was clamped to my ear. I was listening to the broadcast of the seventh game of the 1960 World Series during afternoon recess. My beloved New York Yankees were locked in a death struggle with the Pittsburgh Pirates and the tension was killing me. As bad as it was, I knew it would get worse when the bell rang to summon us back into class. There was no radio playing allowed in school, so, until the end of the day, I'd be in the dark. If I was lucky, if the game lasted long enough and I ran home fast enough, I might catch the last inning on TV.

They played the Series during daylight back then. It was just one of the many ways baseball was different. There were no designated hitters, no costumed mascots, no corporate logos on uniforms, and strikes were something pitchers threw, not walked out on. Those were the glory years. The era was aglitter with stars: Mickey Mantle, Ted Williams, Willie Mays, Hank Aaron, Stan Musial, Roberto Clemente, Frank Robinson, Brooks Robinson, Sandy Koufax, Whitey Ford and Bob Gibson.

There are no rigid timelines for the era. For the purposes of this book I began in 1946, when the big leaguers who had served in the armed forces rejoined their clubs and baseball returned to a semblance of the game it was before the war. I drew the curtain in 1968, the last year the two pennant winners met to decide who would be king. In 1969, both leagues expanded to 12 teams and a league championship series was introduced to determine the Series combatants. Baseball would never be the same again.

In October 1960, I made it home in time to see the last inning of the Series, just in time to watch the Pirates' Bill Mazeroski hit the ball over the wall at Forbes Field and break my heart. It seems like it happened only yesterday.

KERRY BANKS
October 1996

1

Chapter One

AROUND THE HORN

In baseball lingo, an around-the-horn double play occurs when the ball travels from third to second to first. It was originally a nautical term. Prior to the opening of the Panama Canal, the only sailing route from the Atlantic Ocean to the Pacific Ocean was around Cape Horn at the tip of South America. Hence, to go the long way around the diamond was to go around the horn. In this opening chapter we chart a long, meandering route through the glory years, stopping at various ports of call to put you in a mood for nostalgia. *(Answers are on page 8)*

1.1 **With which minor league team did Jackie Robinson make his professional debut on April 18, 1946?**
   A. The Toledo Mud Hens
   B. The Columbus Jets
   C. The Montreal Royals
   D. The Charleston Marlins

1.2 **Which New York Yankee player outpolled Mickey Mantle to win the voting for the 1951 American League Rookie of the Year?**
A. Jackie Jensen
B. Billy Martin
C. Whitey Ford
D. Gil McDougald

1.3 **Who narrowly missed winning a Triple Crown in 1953, when he failed to beat out a ground ball in his last at-bat of the season?**
A. Al Rosen
B. Yogi Berra
C. Eddie Mathews
D. Roy Campanella

1.4 **Who posted the highest single-season batting average from 1946 to 1968?**
A. Stan Musial
B. Ted Williams
C. Mickey Mantle
D. Roberto Clemente

1.5 **Who were the original Whiz Kids?**
A. The 1947 Brooklyn Dodgers
B. The 1950 Philadelphia Phillies
C. The 1959 Chicago White Sox
D. The 1966 Baltimore Orioles

1.6 **Which player had a stint with the Harlem Globetrotters?**
A. Bob Gibson
B. Willie McCovey
C. Vada Pinson
D. Wes Covington

1.7 **Who gave Pete Rose the nickname "Charlie Hustle"?**
A. Ernie Banks
B. Whitey Ford
C. Frank Robinson
D. Casey Stengel

1.8 In 1962, Tommy Davis of the Dodgers topped the National League with a .346 batting average, 230 hits and 153 RBI. Yet Davis did not win the MVP award. It went to another Dodger. Who?

A. Don Drysdale
B. Sandy Koufax
C. Maury Wills
D. Frank Howard

1.9 Which of the following players was not elected to the Hall of Fame in his first year of eligibility?

A. Warren Spahn
B. Joe DiMaggio
C. Lou Brock
D. Brooks Robinson

1.10 How many times between 1946 and 1968 was the National League pennant race decided by a playoff?

A. Two times
B. Three times
C. Four times
D. Five times

1.11 How many intentional walks did Roger Maris receive in 1961, the year he hit 61 homers to break Babe Ruth's record?

A. 0
B. 10
C. 20
D. 40

1.12 In 1949, Jackie Robinson of the Dodgers became the first black player to win an MVP award. In the 19 years from 1949 to 1968, how many times was the National League MVP award won by a black player?

A. Six times
B. Nine times
C. 12 times
D. 15 times

1.13 Who fractured his elbow during the 1950 All-Star game, an injury that cost his team the pennant?
A. Bob Feller
B. Ted Williams
C. Pee Wee Reese
D. Stan Musial

1.14 Which old-time ballpark featured a 40-foot screen in front of the left-field stands, which was dubbed the "Bamboo Curtain"?
A. Sportsman's Park
B. Crosley Field
C. Shibe Park
D. The Los Angeles Coliseum

1.15 Who pitched the longest perfect game in history in 1959, toiling 12 innings without allowing a hit or walk, but still lost the game?
A. Larry Jackson of the Cardinals
B. Joe Nuxhall of the Reds
C. Harvey Haddix of the Pirates
D. Jack Sanford of the Giants

1.16 Who was "Dr. Strangeglove"?
A. Richie Allen
B. Dick Stuart
C. Moose Skowron
D. Marv Throneberry

1.17 Which baseball broadcaster coined the expression, "That ball is going, going, gone!"?
A. Red Barber
b. Harry Caray
C. Mel Allen
D. Ernie Harwell

1.18 In the voting for the 1957 All-Star team, Cincinnati fans stuffed the ballot boxes and helped elect seven Reds to the National League's eight positions. Who was the only player from another team to make the starting lineup?

A. Ernie Banks of the Cubs
B. Hank Aaron of the Braves
C. Stan Musial of the Cardinals
D. Bill Mazeroski of the Pirates

1.19   **In 1963, Major League Baseball changed the size of the strike zone. What were the new dimensions?**
A. Bottom of a batter's knee to his shoulder
B. Bottom of a batter's knee to his armpit
C. Bottom of a batter's knee to his belt buckle
D. Top of a batter's knee to his shoulder

1.20   **Which American League owner tried to install a "pennant porch" during the 1960s?**
A. Dan Topping of the Yankees
B. Bill Veeck of the White Sox
C. Gene Autry of the Angels
D. Charlie Finley of the Athletics

1.21   **Who entered the record books in 1951, by becoming the first AL hurler to register two no-hitters in a season?**
A. Bob Feller of the Indians
B. Allie Reynolds of the Yankees
C. Billy Pierce of the White Sox
D. Mel Parnell of the Red Sox

1.22   **The record for the largest crowd to ever attend a baseball game was set in 1959. What sort of game was it?**
A. A World Series game
B. A playoff game
C. A regular-season game
D. An exhibition game

1.23   **With which team did Duke Snider end his playing career in 1964?**
A. The New York Mets
B. The Los Angeles Dodgers
C. The California Angels
D. The San Francisco Giants

Answers

A R O U N D   T H E   H O R N

1.1 C. The Montreal Royals
Robinson, who had been playing with the Kansas City Monarchs in the Negro Leagues, signed with the Brooklyn Dodgers' farm club, the Montreal Royals, on October 23, 1945. His first game with the Royals was against the Jersey City Giants in Jersey City's Roosevelt Stadium on April 18, 1946. Playing second base, he had a remarkable debut, collecting four hits in five at-bats, including a home run, four RBI and two stolen bases, as the Royals thumped the Giants 14–1. Robinson went on to spark Montreal to the International League pennant, pacing the circuit with a .349 batting average. In the 1946 Junior World Series, Montreal defeated Louisville of the American Association, four games to two, clinching the Series at its home park, Delormier Downs. When Robinson left the stadium after the game, jubilant fans mobbed him and chased him down the street. Sportswriter Sam Maltin noted: "It was probably the only time in history that a black man ran from a white mob with love instead of lynching on its mind."

1.2 D. Gil McDougald
Some Rookie-of-the-Year selections look absurd in hindsight and at first glance the choice of McDougald over Mantle seems to fit the category. But McDougald had the more impressive freshman campaign. The Yankee third baseman hit .306 and topped Mantle in every offensive category except triples and RBI. McDougald continued his sterling play in the post-season, smashing the first grand slam by a rookie in the World Series and leading all players with seven RBI as the Yanks subdued the New York Giants in six games.

1.3   A. Al Rosen

Rosen came to the plate for the final time in 1953, needing one more hit to win the Triple Crown. He knew from a clubhouse radio report that Mickey Vernon of the Washington Senators had collected two hits in four at-bats that day to finish the season with a .337 batting average. Rosen, who had already sewn up the other two hitting categories with 43 homers and 145 RBI, now stood at .336. His last at-bat came against rookie pitcher Al Aber of the Detroit Tigers. Rosen fouled off several pitches, then hit a roller towards third base. He missed beating the throw to first by a half step and lost his bid for the Triple Crown by a single percentage point.

1.4   B. Ted Williams

In 1957, Mickey Mantle and Ted Williams waged a torrid duel for the American League batting title, with Williams finally winning .388 to .365. It was a startling result. Williams was 39 years old, while Mantle was 25 and at the peak of his abilities. A furor erupted when the Baseball Writers of America chose Mantle as MVP, even though Williams had hit more homers and had topped the league in batting average, slugging average and on-base percentage. Incredibly, two writers placed Williams ninth and tenth on their ballots. Obviously, the fact that Mantle's team won the pennant, while the Red Sox finished 16 games back, influenced voters, but Williams's adversarial relationship with the press didn't help his cause.

TOP BATTING AVERAGES (1946–1968)

Player	Year	Team	Average
Ted Williams	1957	Red Sox	.388
Stan Musial	1948	Cardinals	.376
Ted Williams	1948	Red Sox	.369
Mickey Mantle	1957	Yankees	.365
Stan Musial	1946	Cardinals	.365
Harry Walker	1947	Cards/Phillies	.363
Norm Cash	1961	Tigers	.361

1.5   B. The 1950 Philadelphia Phillies

Youthful teams are not supposed to win pennants, but the Phillies confounded the odds, taking the National League title in 1950 with a lineup that averaged 26 years of age, anchored by ace pitchers Robin Roberts (23) and Curt Simmons (21). Some thought the "Whiz Kids" had the makings of a dynasty. But after being swept by the Yankees in the World Series, the Phillies slumped to fifth place in 1951 and never again seriously contended for the pennant for the rest of the decade, earning themselves another nickname— the "Fizz Kids."

1.6   A. Bob Gibson

Watching the great Cardinals pitcher in action one would never guess that he had to overcome an array of childhood ailments, including rickets, asthma and a rheumatic heart, to become a pro athlete. Gibson actually attended Creighton University on a basketball scholarship. After pitching for the Cards' minor league club in Omaha in 1957, he joined the Harlem Globetrotters for a season.

1.7   B. Whitey Ford

During an exhibition game between the Cincinnati Reds and the New York Yankees in Florida in 1963, Mickey Mantle and Whitey Ford were relaxing on the dugout steps when the 21-year-old Rose drew a walk and tore down to first base at full speed. Ford remarked scornfully, "Hey, look at that Charlie Hustle go." The label stuck, and Rose even came to like the name.

1.8   C. Maury Wills

Looking at the numbers today, it is hard to understand how Wills won the National League's MVP award in 1962. The Dodger shortstop hit a paltry six homers and drove in only 48 runs, 105 less than his teammate, Tommy Davis, and a far cry from the stats of the runner-up in the balloting, Willie Mays, who blasted 49 homers and knocked in 141. But time has diminished Wills's revolutionary impact on baseball. During the 1950s, the stolen base had gradually disappeared as an offensive weapon. Wills brought it back in a big way in 1962, swiping 104 bases and breaking Ty Cobb's record of 96, which had been set in 1915. Incredibly, Wills singlehandedly

Hank Aaron: Baseball's all-time home run king.

pilfered more bases than any team in the majors in 1962. With Wills terrorizing the league with his speed, the Dodgers invented a new way to win, manufacturing runs not with booming bats, but rather with dash and daring.

1.9 B. Joe DiMaggio

Amazingly, Joltin' Joe didn't make it into Cooperstown until his third try. Under the rules at the time, he was eligible for induction in 1953, one year after his retirement, but the electors were pre-occupied with the enshrinement of a backlog of old-timers. DiMaggio fell 81 votes short in 1953, finishing eighth in the balloting as Dizzy Dean and Al Simmons collected the majority of votes. In 1954, he was 14 ballots short, as Bill Terry, Rabbit Maranville and Bill Dickey got the nod from the selection committee. After two strikes, DiMaggio finally made it into the Hall in 1955.

1.10 C. Four times

The National League pennant was decided by a best-of-three playoff series in 1946, 1951, 1959 and 1962. In each case, the Dodgers were involved. The Dodgers lost to the Cardinals in 1946 and the Giants in 1951 and 1962, but defeated the Braves in 1959.

1.11 A. 0

Maris profited by batting third in the Yankee lineup in 1961, just ahead of Mickey Mantle. Pitchers did not want to deliberately put Maris on base with Mr. Muscles waiting in the on-deck circle. The numbers bear this out. With Mantle on deck, Maris, in 478 at-bats, had 54 homers, 130 RBI and a .293 batting average. With other Yankees hitting behind him, Maris, in 115 at-bats, had seven homers, 12 RBI and a .174 batting average.

1.12 D. 15 times

The influx of black players into the majors had a terrific impact during the 1950s and 1960s, especially in the National League. Beginning with Jackie Robinson in 1949, black players claimed the National League MVP award 15 times in 19 years. Not surprisingly, it was the Dodgers and the Giants, the two NL clubs that most quickly embraced the integration movement, who became the league powers, while the teams that resisted fell out of contention. When outfielder Richie Ashburn of the Philadelphia Phillies was asked why the Phils never won another pennant after 1950, he answered sagely, "We were all white."

1.13 B. Ted Williams

Williams was injured when he crashed into the outfield wall making a leaping catch of a Ralph Kiner drive in the first inning of the 1950 All-Star game at Comiskey Park. Although in severe pain, he stubbornly played the entire contest, rapping an RBI single in four at-bats. Afterwards, X-rays revealed he had fractured his elbow. The injury forced Williams to miss 60 games and cost Boston the pennant, as the Red Sox finished four games behind the first-place Yankees.

1.14 D. The Los Angeles Coliseum

While waiting for the construction of Dodger Stadium to be completed, the Dodgers played four seasons at the Los Angeles Coliseum, then the home of football's L.A. Rams. Because the left-field stands were a mere 250 feet from home plate, the Dodgers erected a 40-foot-high screen in left that extended 140 feet from the foul pole towards centre field. Initially, there was concern that the Dodgers' righthanded power hitters would make mincemeat of existing home run records, but it didn't turn out that way. Not a single Dodger hit more than 25 homers in a season during the club's stay at the Coliseum. The Bamboo Curtain most benefited lefthanded hitter Wally Moon, who used a patented "inside-out" swing to rattle singles off the barrier and loft fly balls over the screen, which came to be known as "Moon shots."

1.15 C. Harvey Haddix of the Pirates

Haddix pitched the greatest game of all time and didn't even win. Not only that, he was beaten by a home run that wasn't a home run. On May 26, 1959, the veteran lefthander mowed down the Milwaukee Braves' hard-hitting lineup with disdainful ease. After retiring the side 1–2–3 in the bottom of the ninth, Haddix was mobbed by his teammates. He had pitched that rarest of rarities—a perfect game. Unfortunately, the Pirates had not scored a run off Braves pitcher Lew Burdette, and so the game went into extra innings. Haddix set down the Braves in order in the 10th, 11th and 12th. He had dispatched 36 consecutive batters without allowing a hit, walk or error. The game was still scoreless when Felix Mantilla, the Braves' leadoff hitter in the 13th, got on base when third baseman Don Hoak threw wildly to first on a routine grounder. Haddix no longer had a perfect game, but his no-hitter was still intact. Eddie Mathews sacrificed Mantilla to second. Hank Aaron received an intentional walk. Haddix then threw a hanging slider to Joe Adcock, who slammed it over the fence. The no-hitter and the game were lost. That should have been it, but Aaron, unaware that Adcock's drive had cleared the fence, merely touched second and headed for the dugout. By the time anyone noticed, Adcock was on third base. He was declared out for passing a fellow runner on the basepaths. As only Mantilla's run counted, the final score of the game was 1–0. The last word on the bizarre event was left to Burdette, who scattered 12 hits for the victory: "I'm the guy who won the greatest game ever pitched."

1.16 B. Dick Stuart

If he hadn't been such a prodigious slugger, Stuart would never have made the majors. The muscular first sacker was a truly awful fielder, so awful he once received a standing ovation from Pittsburgh fans after scooping up a hot dog wrapper that had blown onto the field. Stuart charted new dimensions in defensive ineptitude. He dropped pop-ups, fumbled grounders, bobbled bunts and missed pickoff throws. In his first seven years in the bigs, Stuart led all first basemen in his league in errors, including his rookie campaign with the Pirates, when he made 16 blunders in only 64 games. In six of those seven years he topped all first sackers in the majors in miscues. His 29 errors in 1963 with the Red Sox nearly tripled that of his nearest competitor. In Beantown he was given another nickname: the Boston Strangler.

1.17 C. Mel Allen

Allen made the auctioneer's call for a home run his signature expression, along with the phrase, "How about that!" Born Melvin Israeli, of Russian immigrant parents in Birmingham, Alabama, he earned a law degree before starting his broadcasting career as the field announcer for University of Alabama football games. Allen will be forever remembered as the "voice of the Yankees," for whom he called games from 1939 to 1964.

1.18   C. Stan Musial of the Cardinals
With the help of broadcaster Waite Hoyt and a city newspaper that printed ballots already filled out and with the address of where to send them, Cincinnati fans sent in a blizzard of ballots and elected eight Reds to the 1957 National League All-Star lineup. The only mystery was how Reds first baseman George Crowe didn't make the team. That spot went to Stan Musial. In response to the ballot-stuffing, commissioner Ford Frick announced that Reds out-fielders Wally Post and Gus Bell would be replaced on the All-Star team by Hank Aaron and Willie Mays. Two other Reds, shortstop Roy McMillan and third baseman Don Hoak, both started, but were removed from the game after one plate appearance. To avoid a repeat incident, Frick decreed that managers and players, and not the fans, would elect the All-Star squads the next season.

1.19   A. Bottom of a batter's knee to his shoulder
The strike zone had previously extended from a batter's armpits to the top of his knee. It was enlarged because baseball's arbiters felt that runs were being scored too easily. By adding an extra few inches they hoped to swing the pendulum back in favour of the pitcher. The move had a more dramatic effect than intended. Home run production in 1963 dropped by 10 per cent and total runs dipped by 12 per cent. Aided by the larger strike zone, pitchers became progressively dominant throughout the decade, until 1969, when the strike zone was reduced to its pre-1963 dimensions and the pitcher's mound was lowered.

1.20   D. Charlie Finley of the Athletics
The A's eccentric owner caused a flap in 1964 with a wacky remodelling scheme. Convinced that the New York Yankees were winning all those AL flags because of the short right-field fence at Yankee Stadium, Finley erected a fence at Kansas City's Municipal Stadium that curved from right-centre field to the foul line, 296

feet from home plate, thus duplicating Yankee Stadium's right-field dimensions. The "pennant porch," as Finley dubbed it, lasted two pre-season games. Commissioner Ford Frick ordered it dismantled, noting that it violated a rule for stadiums built after 1958, which required they extend at least 325 feet down the foul lines. Finley responded by erecting a "one-half pennant porch," 325 feet from the plate, which he kept in place for 1964 and 1965. Kansas City's home run total jumped dramatically, but the increased power output didn't bring the A's any closer to a pennant. They finished dead last.

1.21 B. Allie Reynolds of the Yankees

The Yankee righthander fired his first no-hitter on July 12, 1951, against Cleveland. Reynolds's second gem, versus Boston on September 28, was more dramatic. Not only did the victory clinch a share of the pennant for the Yanks, but the last batter he faced in the game was Ted Williams. Challenging Williams with fastballs, Reynolds got the Boston slugger to hit a pop fly behind the plate. Catcher Yogi Berra drifted back, got under the ball—and then dropped it, causing some 40,000 Yankee fans to groan in unison. Undeterred, Reynolds induced Williams to pop up again. This time, Berra caught the ball.

1.22 D. An exhibition game

A crowd of 93,103—the largest ever to watch a baseball game—turned out on May 7, 1959 for an exhibition contest between the Dodgers and the Yankees at the Los Angeles Coliseum. The game was staged as a tribute to ex-Dodger catcher Roy Campanella, who had been confined to a wheelchair after a 1958 automobile accident.

1.23 D. The San Francisco Giants

Ironically, Snider ended his career in 1964, playing in the outfield alongside Willie Mays in a Giants uniform—the club that had been the Dodgers' most bitter rival during Snider's heyday with Brooklyn in the 1950s.

WILLIE, MICKEY & THE DUKE

During the 1950s, New York boasted baseball's three best centre fielders: Willie Mays of the Giants, Mickey Mantle of the Yankees and Duke Snider of the Dodgers. In this game, your task is to match the member of this talented trio with his achievement.

(Answers are on page 137)

1. _____ was voted Rookie of the Year.

2. _____ twice hit four homers in a World Series.

3. _____ won three MVP awards.

4. _____ topped the 100-RBI mark 10 times.

5. _____ hit 40-plus homers five straight years.

6. _____ won 12 Gold Glove awards.

7. _____ won a Triple Crown.

8. _____ once stole 40 bases in a season.

9. _____ hit four homers in one game.

10. _____ spent his entire career in the outfield.

11. _____ led his league in runs scored six times.

12. _____ hit homers in three All-Star games.

Chapter Two

THE LUMBERYARD

In the 1950s, baseball became an increasingly one-dimensional game. Offensive strategy was built around one central idea: get runners on base and hit home runs. Muscles came to matter more than speed. In 1943, the 16 clubs in the majors collected 905 homers and 1,010 stolen bases. In 1955, they combined for 2,224 homers and 694 stolen bases. It's no wonder that one of the era's most popular television shows was "Home Run Derby."

(Answers are on page 24)

2.1 **Which MVP led his club to a pennant by hitting .523 with five homers and 16 RBI during the final two weeks of the season, including seven hits in eight at-bats in his team's last two games?**
A. Jackie Robinson in 1949
B. Hank Aaron in 1957
C. Ken Boyer in 1964
D. Carl Yastrzemski in 1967

2.2 **When he retired after the 1968 season, where did Mickey Mantle rank on the career home run list?**
A. First
B. Second
C. Third
D. Fourth

2.3 **Who hit the most homers in the majors during the 1950s?**
A. Willie Mays
B. Duke Snider
C. Mickey Mantle
D. Gil Hodges

2.4 **What did Eddie Mathews accomplish in 1953 that no other player has ever duplicated?**
A. He belted two grand slams in one game
B. He reached the 45-homer plateau at age 21
C. He swatted 19 home runs in one month
D. He hit homers in his first two at-bats in the majors

2.5 **Who was the only player of the era to hit four consecutive home runs in a game?**
A. Willie McCovey
B. Ernie Banks
C. Rocky Colavito
D. Ted Williams

2.6 **Who hit the most homers in the majors during the 1960s?**
A. Hank Aaron
B. Willie Mays
C. Frank Robinson
D. Harmon Killebrew

2.7 **Who tied the NL mark for most homers by a rookie in 1956?**
A. Hank Aaron
B. Frank Robinson
C. Bill White
D. Bobby Del Greco

2.8 In which of the following offensive categories did Willie Mays
not lead the NL during any season of his career?

A. Hits

B. Runs scored

C. Runs batted in

D. Batting average

2.9 Which slugger was pitcher Curt Simmons referring to when he
said:"Trying to sneak a fastball past him is like trying to sneak a
sunrise past a rooster"?

A. Hank Aaron

B. Willie Mays

C. Richie Allen

D. Roy Campanella

2.10 In five of 23 seasons between 1946 and 1968, no National
Leaguer reached the 200-hit mark. How many times did the
American League fail to produce a 200-hit man?

A. Four times

B. Seven times

C. 10 times

D. 13 times

2.11 Who was the only player of the era to collect more than 100
extra-base hits in a season?

A. Stan Musial

B. Hank Aaron

C. Willie Mays

D. Frank Robinson

2.12 Who edged Ted Williams for the American League batting title
by .00016 of a percentage point in 1949, to prevent Williams
from winning an unprecedented third Triple Crown?

A. George Kell of the Tigers

B. Luke Appling of the White Sox

C. Ferris Fain of the Athletics

D. Dale Mitchell of the Indians

2.13 Who established a major league first when he clubbed 40 or more homers, while striking out 40 or fewer times, in three consecutive seasons during the 1950s?
A. Eddie Mathews
B. Duke Snider
C. Ted Williams
D. Ted Kluszewski

2.14 Aside from 1961, when he blasted 61 homers, what was the most round-trippers Roger Maris hit in a season?
A. 29
B. 39
C. 49
D. 59

2.15 Whose 10th-inning homer in the last game of the 1950 season clinched the Philadelphia Phillies' first pennant since 1915?
A. Del Ennis
B. Dick Sisler
C. Richie Ashburn
D. Granny Hamner

2.16 Which two players were separated by a single vote in the balloting for MVP honours?
A. Joe DiMaggio and Ted Williams in 1947
B. Roy Campanella and Duke Snider in 1955
C. Hank Aaron and Stan Musial in 1957
D. Roger Maris and Mickey Mantle in 1960

2.17 What was unusual about the American League batting title that Billy Goodman won in 1950?
A. Goodman was a utility player
B. Goodman did not hit a single home run
C. Goodman played for two teams that year
D. Goodman retired before the end of the season

2.18 How many homers did Roger Maris hit on the road, as compared to at Yankee Stadium, in 1961?

Cleveland's Al Rosen: AL MVP in 1953.

A. 21 on the road, 40 at home
B. 26 on the road, 35 at home
C. 31 on the road, 30 at home
D. 36 on the road, 25 at home

2.19   How many different players hit 50 or more homers in a season during the era?
A. Three
B. Five
C. Seven
D. Nine

2.20   Who was the first rookie in the 20th century to win a major league batting crown?
A. Tony Oliva
B. Al Kaline
C. Pete Rose
D. Richie Allen

Answers

THE LUMBERYARD

2.1 **D. Carl Yastrzemski in 1967**

In Boston, 1967 is remembered as the "Year of the Yaz." The 27-year-old outfielder carried the Red Sox on his back, hitting .326 with 44 homers and 121 RBI to claim the American League's Triple Crown and MVP award. "Yaz probably meant 30 victories to us," said Boston skipper Dick Williams, "maybe 20 with his bat and another 10 with his arm." After finishing ninth the previous year, Boston was a 100-to-one shot to win the pennant at the start of 1967. The race came down to the final weekend, with the Red Sox sweeping the Minnesota Twins in their final two contests to take the flag by a single game. Yastrzemski came up big as usual, rapping seven hits in eight at-bats in the do-or-die series.

2.2 **C. Third**

When Mantle called it quits after the 1968 season, he ranked third on the career home run list behind Babe Ruth and Willie Mays. Mantle's chronic leg miseries caused him to consider retiring after 1967, but he opted to play one more season with the intention of passing Ted Williams (521) and Jimmy Foxx (534) on the homer chart. Though he succeeded, he later regretted the effort because he hit only .237, which caused his career batting average to dip below .300 to .298. As of 1996, Mantle's career total of 536 homers was the eighth best of all time.

2.3 **B. Duke Snider**

Although he led the National League in homers only once during the 1950s, the Duke of Flatbush was the decade's home run king by a comfortable margin. Snider's forte was his consistency. He went deep 40 times or more five straight seasons from 1953 to 1957. There is no doubt he was aided by Ebbets Field's cozy dimensions. When the Dodgers moved west in 1958 and took up residence in the Los Angeles Memorial Coliseum, with its spacious right field, Snider's home run production plummeted.

TOP HOME RUN HITTERS OF THE 1950S

Player	Team	HR
Duke Snider	Dodgers	326
Gil Hodges	Dodgers	310
Eddie Mathews	Braves	299
Mickey Mantle	Yankees	280
Stan Musial	Cardinals	266
Yogi Berra	Yankees	256
Willie Mays	Giants	250

2.4   B. He reached the 45-homer plateau at age 21
Mathews dialed long distance 47 times for the Milwaukee Braves in 1953. No one so young has ever stroked so many homers in a season. The 135 ribbies that the 21-year-old amassed in 1953 is also an NL record for hot-corner performers. The pull-hitting Texan would go on to rack up 512 career homers, second only to Mike Schmidt among third basemen.

2.5   C. Rocky Colavito
The Cleveland Indians' slugger cleared the fences four times in four consecutive trips to the plate against the Baltimore Orioles on June 10, 1959. Colavito hit a third-inning shot off pitcher Jerry Walker, fifth- and sixth-inning drives off Arnold Portocarrero and a ninth-inning blast off Ernie Johnson as the Indians posted an 11–8 victory. Colavito's feat was especially remarkable because it occurred in one of the toughest home run hitting parks in the majors. Prior to Colavito's barrage, Baltimore's Memorial Stadium had not yielded more than three homers to a team in one game.

2.6 **D. Harmon Killebrew**

The leading fence-buster of the 1960s was called "Killer." The nickname referred to Killebrew's destructive bat and not his personality. The mild-mannered country boy from Payette, Idaho, put 393 baseballs into the seats during the decade. Many of his blasts were tape-measure shots. As Baltimore Orioles manager Paul Richards noted: "Killebrew can knock the ball out of any park, including Yellowstone."

TOP HOME RUN HITTERS OF THE 1960S

Player	Team	HR
Harmon Killebrew	Senators/Twins	393
Hank Aaron	Braves	375
Willie Mays	Giants	350
Frank Robinson	Reds/Orioles	316
Willie McCovey	Giants	300
Frank Howard	Dodgers/Senators	288
Norm Cash	Tigers	278

2.7 **B. Frank Robinson**

The hard-hitting native of Beaumont, Texas, gave Cincinnati fans a hint of what lay in store in the future in 1956, when he blasted 38 homers in his rookie season, tying Wally Berger's 1930 mark for the most by a National League freshman. Robinson's first-year performance was so impressive he was a unanimous selection as the NL Rookie of the Year.

2.8 **C. Runs batted in**

Mays paced the National League in hits in 1960, in runs in 1958 and 1961, and in batting average in 1954, but he never topped the loop in runs batted in. He finished second twice, behind Duke Snider in 1955 and Tommy Davis in 1962. This is partly due to the fact that Mays batted third in the Giants' batting order for much of his career, rather than in the cleanup spot, but it also underscores the high calibre of hitters he had to compete with in the NL.

2.9 **A. Hank Aaron**

A pair of amazingly quick, strong wrists and a keen batting eye gave Hammerin' Hank an edge over other hitters. As Aaron noted: "I never worried about the fastball. They couldn't throw it past me. None of them." Because he hit the heater so well, Aaron could afford to go up to the plate looking for breaking balls. The technique helped him compile an all-time record of 755 homers.

2.10 **D. 13 times**

Although the National League is perceived to have had superior pitching during the era, this stat indicates that the American Leaguers were having more trouble making contact with the ball. In only 10 of the era's 23 seasons did an AL player reach 200 hits. From 1956 to 1968, only Bobby Richardson (1961) and Tony Oliva (1964) topped the mark. A contributing factor was the junior circuit's reluctance to sign black ballplayers, an oversight that gave the NL a marked edge in talent.

2.11 **A. Stan Musial**

The number of doubles, triples and homers a player hits in a season is a good indicator of all-around power, and there were few better all-around power hitters than Stan Musial. Entering the 1997 season, only eight players in history had collected 100 extra-base hits or more in a season, and since 1937 just two have managed the feat: Musial (103 in 1948) and Albert Belle (103 in 1995).

MOST EXTRA-BASE HITS IN A SEASON (1946–1968)

Player	Year	2B	3B	HR	Total
Stan Musial	1948	46	18	39	103
Stan Musial	1953	53	9	30	92
Hank Aaron	1959	46	7	39	92
Frank Robinson	1962	51	2	39	92
Stan Musial	1949	41	13	36	90
Willie Mays	1962	36	5	49	90
Duke Snider	1954	39	10	40	89

2.12   **A. George Kell of the Tigers**
Kell entered the last game of the 1949 season against Cleveland
trailing Ted Williams by two percentage points in the batting race.
But more was at stake for Williams than the batting title. Not only
was he in a position to claim a third Triple Crown, the Red Sox
and the Yankees were meeting in a game to decide the pennant.
Williams walked twice and went 0 for 2 at the plate as the Yanks
beat the BoSox to take the flag. Kell, who was 2 for 3 on the day,
was due up in the ninth inning against Cleveland when word
reached the dugout that Williams had gone hitless in New York.
Tiger manager Red Rolfe offered to send in a pinch-hitter, telling
Kell. "If you don't bat, you win it." Kell bravely opted to take his
place in the on-deck circle. There was a runner on first and one
out. Shortstop Eddie Lake grounded into a game-ending double
play and the batting title belonged to Kell.

2.13   **D. Ted Kluszewski**
Only five players—Joe DiMaggio, Lou Gehrig, Johnny Mize, Mel
Ott and Ted Kluszewski—have hit 40 or more homers and struck
out 40 or fewer times in a season. Amazingly, Kluszewski did it
three times! The Cincinnati Reds slugger belted 40 homers in
1953, 49 in 1954 and 47 in 1955. His strikeout totals for those
years were 34, 35 and 40. That's 136 homers and only 109 strikeouts for the three-year span, quite a departure from the typical
all-or-nothing image of a long-ball hitter.

40 HOMERS OR MORE/40 STRIKEOUTS OR LESS

Player	Year	Team	HR	SO
Lou Gehrig	1934	Yankees	49	31
Ted Kluszewski	1954	Reds	49	35
Ted Kluszewski	1955	Reds	47	40
Joe DiMaggio	1937	Yankees	46	37
Mel Ott	1929	Giants	42	38
Ted Kluszewski	1953	Reds	40	34
Johnny Mize	1948	Giants	40	37

Mickey Mantle connects in 1961.

2.14 **B. 39**

Maris never came close to matching his 1961 power surge. The 61 homers he hit that year represent 22 per cent of his career total of 275. His next best performance was in 1960, when he hit 39 homers, one less than the AL leader, Mickey Mantle.

2.15 **B. Dick Sisler**

Sisler's dramatic, three-run blast into the left-field stands at Ebbets Field broke up a tense 1–1 pitching duel between the Dodgers' Don Newcombe and the Phillies' Robin Roberts. When Brooklyn failed to score in the bottom of the tenth, the jubilant Phillies poured onto the field to celebrate their first pennant in 35 years.

2.16 **A. Joe DiMaggio and Ted Williams in 1947**

Roger Maris edged Mickey Mantle for AL MVP honours by just three votes in 1960, but that still wasn't quite as close as the 1947 balloting. Much has been made of the fact that Williams lost by a single vote because a Boston writer named Del Webb left the Red Sox star entirely off his ballot. But Bill James points out in his *Historical Baseball Abstract* that three voters omitted DiMaggio's name from their ballots. Statistically, Williams outdistanced DiMaggio in virtually every offensive category, as the Red Sox star led the AL in batting average, homers, RBI, slugging average and total bases. But the MVP award usually goes to a player from a pennant winner and DiMaggio's club finished first while Williams's was third.

2.17 **A. Goodman was a utility player**

Goodman had been the Boston Red Sox's first baseman in 1948 and 1949, but he did not really suit the position, which is normally reserved for long-ball threats, having hit only one home run in the two years. In 1950, the Red Sox gave the first-base job to promising rookie slugger Walt Dropo. Unable to find a spot elsewhere, Goodman ended up playing 45 games in the outfield, 27 at third, 21 at first, five at second and one at shortstop. It was only after Ted Williams was injured in mid-season that Goodman got steady playing time in left field and racked up enough plate apearances to qualify for the batting title, which he won with a .354 average.

2.18   C. 31 on the road, 30 at home

People seeking to diminish Maris's accomplishment often claim that he hit 61 homers in 1961 only because of all the cheapies he pulled down the line into the 296-foot right-field porch at Yankee Stadium. In truth, Maris actually hit more homers on the road in 1961. Maris may have jerked a few shots into the right-field seats at Yankee Stadium, but then so did the Bambino when he hit 60 in 1927. Maris's mark has now lasted 35 years—longer than Ruth's did.

2.19   B. Five

Five players topped the 50-home run mark during the era. Roger Maris and Mickey Mantle were the only two American Leaguers to manage it, while Willie Mays, Ralph Kiner and Johnny Mize were the three National Leaguers who reached the elite circle.

THE 50-HOME RUN CLUB (1946–68)

Player	Year	Team	HR
Roger Maris	1961	Yankees	61
Mickey Mantle	1961	Yankees	54
Ralph Kiner	1949	Pirates	54
Mickey Mantle	1956	Yankees	52
Willie Mays	1965	Giants	52
Willie Mays	1955	Giants	51
Ralph Kiner	1947	Pirates	51
Johnny Mize	1947	Giants	51

2.20   A. Tony Oliva

In 1964, Oliva hit .323 to become the only rookie in the 20th century to win a major league batting title. The Cuban also accomplished something nearly as rare by topping the American League in total bases. His total of 374 tied Hal Trosky's 1934 mark for the most ever by a rookie. Not surprisingly, Oliva was voted AL Rookie of the Year.

BY ANY OTHER NAME

PART I

The best nicknames not only sound good, they also reveal something about a player's appearance or style of play. Match each of these nicknames with the correct player.   *(Answers are on page 137)*

1. _____ Cha Cha		A. Whitey Ford
2. _____ Slick		B. Frank Howard
3. _____ Killer		C. Brooks Robinson
4. _____ Bullet		D. Ken Harrelson
5. _____ Hondo		E. Willie McCovey
6. _____ Hawk		F. Vernon Law
7. _____ Kitten		G. Phil Rizzuto
8. _____ Stretch		H. Bob Turley
9. _____ Hoover		I. Harvey Haddix
10. _____ Flip		J. Harmon Killebrew
11. _____ Deacon		K. Al Rosen
12. _____ Scooter		L. Orlando Cepeda

PART II

Some monikers are so familiar we tend to forget that they are nicknames. Match each of these well-known baseball men with the names that appear on their birth certificates.

1. _____ Duke Snider   A. Harold

2. _____ Yogi Berra   B. William

3. _____ Red Schoendienst   C. Fred

4. _____ Boog Powell   D. Leroy

5. _____ Pee Wee Reese   E. Forrest

6. _____ Dixie Walker   F. John

7. _____ Moose Skowron   G. Edwin

8. _____ Casey Stengel   H. Albert

9. _____ Smoky Burgess   I. James

10. _____ Satchel Paige   J. Lawrence

11. _____ Dusty Rhodes   K. George

12. _____ Birdie Tebbetts   L. Charles

Chapter Three

THROWING HEAT

I n 1946, Wheaties, "the breakfast of champions," offered Bob Feller $5,000 if he could break Rube Waddell's single-season strikeout record. Feller asked the league office what the record was. He was told it was 343. Rapid Robert went on to whiff 348 batters. However, after the season, the league admitted it had made a mistake. Upon a review of the data, it was determined that Waddell had actually fanned 349. Feller never approached the mark again, but he had set the tone for the era. As power hitters stole the offensive spotlight, power pitchers responded in kind, by throwing heat.

(Answers are on page 40)

3.1 **Who was Richie Ashburn talking about, when he said: "Either he throws the fastest ball I've ever seen, or I'm going blind."**
A. Bob Gibson
B. Don Drysdale
C. Sandy Koufax
D. Jim Maloney

3.2 Which notorious spitballer was sportswriter Red Smith referring
to, when he said, "The papers needed three columns for his
pitching record: "Won, lost and relative humidity"?
A. Lew Burdette of the Braves
B. Ruben Gomez of the Giants
C. Bob Lemon of the Indians
D. Billy Pierce of the White Sox

3.3 Which rookie fanned a frosh record 245 batters in 1955, to
become the first pitcher to average more than one strikeout
per inning?
A. Johnny Antonelli
B. Bob Turley
C. Herb Score
D. Billy Hoeft

3.4 Sandy Koufax notched 300 strikeouts or more three times. How
many other hurlers topped 300 Ks during the era?
A. One
B. Two
C. Three
D. Four

3.5 Who was the only pitcher from the era to lead his league in wins
five years in a row?
A. Warren Spahn
B. Robin Roberts
C. Whitey Ford
D. Sandy Koufax

3.6 In 1968, Bob Gibson won the National League Cy Young award,
posting 13 shutouts and a 1.12 ERA, the third-best in major
league history. What was Gibson's win-loss record?
A. 19–12
B. 22–9
C. 25–6
D. 28–3

3.7   Only once in the majors has a pitching staff recorded more
strikeouts than hits allowed. Which club owns the mark?

A. The 1964 Cincinnati Reds

B. The 1965 Los Angeles Dodgers

C. The 1966 Baltimore Orioles

D. The 1968 Cleveland Indians

3.8   What did New York Giants pitcher Hoyt Wilhelm do in 1952 that
has never been duplicated?

A. Issued 185 bases on balls

B. Won an ERA crown without starting a single game

C. Tossed shutouts in both ends of a doubleheader

D. Fanned nine batters in a row

3.9   The individual pitching records listed below were all shattered
during the 1960s. Which one had existed the longest?

A. Most consecutive ERA titles

B. Most strikeouts in a World Series game

C. Most consecutive scoreless innings pitched

D. Most strikeouts in a season

3.10   Who was the only pitcher of the era to win a game for the
Yankees in the post-season and beat the Yankees in Series play
with another team?

A. Joe Page

B. Sal Maglie

C. Johnny Sain

D. Don Larsen

3.11   Sandy Koufax won 165 games during his 12-year career. How
many wins did Koufax have after his first six seasons?

A. 16

B. 36

C. 56

D. 76

3.12 **Pittsburgh Pirates relief ace Elroy Face baffled batters with what pitch in the 1950s and 1960s?**
A. The screwball
B. The slider
C. The knuckleball
D. The forkball

3.13 **Which hurler limited opposition hitters to a collective batting average of .168, the lowest in major league history?**
A. Herb Score in 1956
B. Sandy Koufax in 1965
C. Bob Gibson in 1968
D. Luis Tiant in 1968

3.14 **Why was Sal Maglie called "the Barber"?**
A. Because his real name was Barberino
B. Because he owned a barbershop
C. Because he was never clean-shaven
D. Because he often threw the ball close to batters' chins

3.15 **Which pitcher was known as "the Yankee killer"?**
A. Pedro Ramos
B. Steve Barber
C. Frank Lary
D. Mudcat Grant

3.16 **Who won 25 games or more three times, yet never won the Cy Young award?**
A. Jim Kaat
B. Whitey Ford
C. Juan Marichal
D. Don Drysdale

3.17 **Who gave up Roger Maris's record-breaking 61st home run?**
A. Paul Foytack of the Tigers
B. Barry Latman of the Indians
C. Tracy Stallard of the Red Sox
D. Chuck Estrada of the Orioles

3.18 How old was Satchel Paige when he made his last pitching appearance in the majors?
A. 49
B. 54
C. 59
D. 64

3.19 Who shut out the National League champion Los Angeles Dodgers all five times he faced them in 1966?
A. Gaylord Perry of the Giants
B. Ken Holtzman of the Cubs
C. Larry Jaster of the Cardinals
D. Chris Short of the Phillies

3.20 Of the pitchers who won 20 games or more during the era, who posted the best single-season winning percentage?
A. Preacher Roe of the 1951 Dodgers
B. Whitey Ford of the 1961 Yankees
C. Sandy Koufax of the 1963 Dodgers
D. Denny McLain of the 1968 Tigers

3.21 Who was the only pitcher besides Sandy Koufax to win the Cy Young award between 1963 and 1966?
A. Don Drysdale
B. Gary Peters
C. Dean Chance
D. Whitey Ford

Answers

THROWING HEAT

3.1   C. Sandy Koufax

For a lefthanded hitter like Ashburn, Koufax's southpaw delivery must have been especially unnerving. Koufax once described pitching as "the art of instilling fear," and with his explosive fastball and hellacious curve, he could turn even the toughest hitter's knees to jelly. The Dodger flamethrower dominated the National League from 1962 to 1966, hurling four no-hitters, capturing five straight ERA titles and winning three Cy Young awards (at a time when the award was given only to the best pitcher in both leagues). A chronic arm problem forced Koufax to retire at age 30. Had he stayed healthy for a few more years, there is no telling what he might have accomplished.

3.2   A. Lew Burdette of the Braves

During the 1950s, Burdette was often accused of using the damp delivery, though he always denied doing anything illegal. "My best pitch is the one I don't throw," he said cryptically. Eventually, Burdette's non-existent spitter became such a running joke that rival players would take the balls he was throwing and write on them: "Spit here, Lew."

3.3   C. Herb Score

In 1955, the Cleveland Indians added a 22-year-old lefthander to their pitching corps, who was billed as the successor to Bob Feller. His name was Herb Score. In his first season, Score used a blazing fastball and sharp-breaking curve to win 16 games and strike out 245 batters, setting a new rookie record. In his sophomore year in

1956, he fanned 263, won 20 games and appeared to be a Hall of Famer in the making. But early in the 1957 campaign, Score was hit in the eye by a line drive off the bat of Yankee Gil McDougald. The southpaw was lucky not to lose his eye. He recovered from the injury to play five more seasons, but the magic was gone. In 1962, at age 29, Score retired with a career record of 55 wins and 46 losses.

3.4 B. Two

If you read the chapter introduction you know that Bob Feller notched 348 strikeouts in 1946. But there was another Cleveland Indians pitcher who also surpassed 300 Ks: Sam McDowell. In 1965, at age 22, Sudden Sam whiffed 325 batters in 273 innings, to become the youngest pitcher to register 300 strikeouts in a season. The southpaw's ratio of 10.71 strikeouts per nine innings also set a new major league record. Blowing away hitters with his high gas, McDowell won 17 games for the sixth-place Indians and led the AL with a 2.18 ERA.

3.5 A. Warren Spahn

Spahn either led or tied for the National League lead in wins five straight years from 1957 to 1961. Even more amazing, he did it in his late thirties, when one would expect his skills to be eroding. But Spahn seemed ageless. In 1963, at age 42, he won 23 games, the highest total of his career, and just two less than NL leaders Sandy Koufax and Juan Marichal, two elite pitchers in their prime. In all, Spahn paced the NL in victories a record eight times during his 21-year career.

3.6 B. 22–9

Gibson's sizzling performance ranks among the greatest of all-time. In his 34 starts in 1968, he pitched 28 complete games, including 13 shutouts. In nine games he allowed opponents just one run. In the six games he didn't finish, he was removed for pinch-hitters— he was never knocked out of the box. So why did Gibson only win 22 games, and how did he lose nine times? Since 13 of Gibson's wins came via shutouts, his record was a mediocre 9–9 in games in which he didn't whitewash the opposition. Yet, even if you delete his 13 shutouts, his ERA works out to a sparkling 1.53, still the best in the league by a wide margin. In 1968, the Cards scored an average of 3.6 runs per game, two runs a game better than Gibson's ERA. The only explanation we are left with is that the Redbirds' bats went into hibernation whenever Gibson was pitching. With a bit more offensive support, he could have won 30 games.

3.7   D. The 1968 Cleveland Indians

When you consider that many Hall of Famers, including Whitey Ford, Warren Spahn, Robin Roberts and Early Wynn, never once recorded more strikeouts than hits allowed in a season, you gain a greater appreciation of the incredible dominance of the 1968 Indians pitching staff. Led by Luis Tiant, Sam McDowell and Sonny Siebert, Cleveland hurlers fanned a total of 1,157 batters, while allowing only 1,087 hits. With those numbers, it's difficult to fathom how the Tribe finished 17 games out of first.

3.8   B. Won an ERA crown without starting a single game

After a long climb through the minors, Wilhelm debuted with the New York Giants in 1951 as a 28-year-old rookie. The knuckleball specialist had an immediate impact. He pitched 159 innings in 71 games, all in relief, posting a win-loss record of 15–3, with 11 saves and a league-leading ERA of 2.43. No other pitcher has ever won an ERA title while used exclusively as a reliever, primarily because it is so difficult to work enough innings to qualify. Oddly, Wilhelm was not voted the NL Rookie of the Year. The honour went to another reliever, Joe Black of the Dodgers, who was 15–4 with 15 saves and a 2.15 ERA. However, Black was 10 innings shy of qualifying for the ERA crown.

3.9   D. Most strikeouts in a season

Rube Waddell's 1904 mark of 349 strikeouts lasted 61 years before Sandy Koufax finally broke it in 1965. Walter Johnson's 1913 record of 56 scoreless innings was snapped by Don Drysdale in 1968, a span of 55 years. Sandy Koufax eclipsed Lefty Grove's 1932 record of four consecutive ERA titles with his fifth in a row in 1966, a gap of 34 years. Carl Erskine's 1953 record of 14 strikeouts in a World Series game, fell to Koufax when he fanned 15 Yankees in the 1963 Series, a span of 10 years.

Pitcher Don Gibson: He took no prisoners.

3.10 D. Don Larsen

Larsen appeared in four World Series with the Yankees, winning games in 1956, 1957 and 1958. In 1962, he made a return to the Fall Classic, but this time with the San Francisco Giants. Larsen made three relief appearances against his former team and picked up the victory in game four to earn the distinction of being the only pitcher from the era to win a post-season game with the Yankees and then beat them in the Series with another club.

3.11 B. 36

It is often forgotten that Sandy Koufax compiled an anemic 36–40 win-loss record in his first six seasons. He could always throw hard, but early in his career he had little control and even less savvy. If Koufax had been allowed a few years to perfect his mechanics in the minors, he might have made an impact earlier in his career, but he was prevented from doing so by a legal technicality. Koufax signed with the Dodgers for a $20,000 bonus in 1955, and the rules at the time mandated that any player who had received a signing bonus of more than $6,000 had to remain with his big league club for two years. It wasn't until 1961 that Koufax finally stopped overthrowing and found his rhythm, much to the chagrin of NL hitters.

THE KOUFAX CHRONICLES

First Six Seasons				Second Six Seasons			
Year	W	L	ERA	Year	W	L	ERA
1955	2	2	3.02	1961	18	13	3.52
1956	2	4	4.91	1962	14	7	2.54
1957	5	4	3.88	1963	25	5	1.88
1958	11	11	4.48	1964	19	5	1.74
1959	8	6	4.05	1965	26	8	2.04
1960	8	13	3.91	1966	27	9	1.73
Total	36	40			129	47	

3.12 D. The forkball

At five foot eight, Elroy Face lacked the size and strength to overpower hitters with speed, so he resorted to deception. His bread-and-butter pitch was the forkball. To throw it, Face wedged the ball between his index and middle fingers and released it with a strong wrist snap. The result was an off-speed pitch that broke sharply downward as it neared the plate. With his trick pitch, Face led the NL in saves three times. In 1959, he used it to win 17 games in a row, finishing with an astounding 18–1 mark. Face's forkball would later become an effective weapon for many other pitchers, who dubbed it a "split-finger fastball."

3.13 **D. Luis Tiant in 1968**

In 1968, the Cuban dervish faced 905 hitters (not counting walks, sacrifices and hit batsmen) and allowed only 152 hits. That's a combined batting average of just .168. Tiant's phenomenal effort broke the record of .176 set by Ed Reulbach of the Chicago Cubs in 1906. No pitcher has surpassed Tiant's mark, though Nolan Ryan came close, limiting the opposition to averages of .171 in 1972, and .172 in 1991.

LOWEST OPPONENTS' BATTING AVERAGES (1946–68)

Pitcher	Year	Team	W–L	OBA
Luis Tiant	1968	Indians	21–9	.168
Sandy Koufax	1965	Dodgers	26–8	.179
Dave McNally	1968	Orioles	22–10	.182
Tommy Byrne	1949	Yankees	15–7	.183
Bob Gibson	1968	Cardinals	22–9	.184
Al Downing	1963	Yankees	13–5	.184
Sam McDowell	1965	Indians	17–11	.185
Herb Score	1956	Indians	20–9	.186

3.14 **D. Because he often threw the ball close to batters' chins**

A mainstay of the New York Giants mound corps in the 1950s, Maglie was known for his meanness. On the topic of deliberately throwing brushback pitches, he once said: "It's not the first one. It's the second one that makes the hitter know I meant the first one."

3.15 **C. Frank Lary**

The hard-throwing native of Northport, Alabama, displayed a mysterious mastery over New York during his career, beating them 27 times against 13 losses. Lary established himself as the Yankees' arch-nemesis when he was with the Detroit Tigers in the late 1950s. In 1958 and 1959, he won 12 of 13 decisions against New York, including seven wins in 1958 alone, the first time a pitcher had beaten the Yanks seven times in a season since 1918.

3.16 C. Juan Marichal

In another era, Marichal likely would have won three Cy Young awards, but the Dominican Dandy had the misfortune of having his best seasons in years when other pitchers performed even more brilliantly. In 1963, when Marichal was 25–8 with 2.41 ERA, the Cy Young winner was Sandy Koufax, who was 25–5 with a 1.88 ERA. In 1966, when Marichal was 25–6 with a 2.23 ERA, he lost again to Koufax, who was 27–9 with 1.73 ERA. In 1968, when Marichal was 26–9 with a 2.43 ERA, the award went to Bob Gibson, who was 22–9 with a 1.12 ERA.

3.17 C. Tracy Stallard of the Red Sox

Roger Maris clouted his historic home run number 61 off Stallard in the fourth inning of the final game of the 1961 season. The 23-year-old Red Sox rookie told reporters after the game, "I have nothing to be ashamed of. He hit 60 others didn't he?"

3.18 C. 59

Paige had been out of the majors since 1953, when Charlie Finley, the owner of the Kansas City Athletics, decided to bring back the ageless wonder for one last appearance in 1965. Finley's main motivation was creating publicity, but Paige appreciated the gesture. Despite his age, he twirled three scoreless innings against the Boston Red Sox, allowing only one hit. As Mark Ribowsky recounts in his book *Don't Look Back*, "Before the next inning, Paige went out to the hill again, to be removed according to plan by manager Haywood Sullivan. He doffed his cap and disappeared into the dugout. Outside, the stadium lights were doused and the PA announcer instructed the fans to light matches and cigarette lighters in the dark and sing along to "The Old Gray Mare."

3.19 C. Larry Jaster of the Cardinals

Jaster won only 11 games in 1966, but he deep-sixed the NL champion Dodgers five times in five starts, shutting them out each time. No other pitcher has ever posted five consecutive shutouts against one club in a season. Oddly, those were the only shutouts Jaster recorded in 1966. In fact, he pitched only two more in his entire seven-year career.

3.20 **A. Preacher Roe of the 1951 Dodgers**

In 1951, the Dodger lefty went 22–3 for an .880 winning percentage—the highest ever by a 20-game winner in the NL. Roe, who
compiled a .715 winning percentage in seven years for the Dodgers
without the aid of an effective fastball, said his repertoire consisted
of three pitches: "My change, my change off my change, and my
change off my change off my change." Opposition players insisted
there was another pitch that belonged on the list: the spitball. After
he retired in 1955, Roe admitted in a *Sports Illustrated* article that
he had indeed been throwing a spitter as his money pitch, a con-
fession that set off a major furor.

TOP WINNING PCT. BY 20-GAME WINNERS (1946–68)

Player	Year	Team	W	L	Pct.
Preacher Roe	1951	Dodgers	22	3	.880
Whitey Ford	1961	Yankees	25	4	.862
Denny McLain	1968	Tigers	31	6	.838
Sandy Koufax	1963	Dodgers	25	5	.833
Bob Purkey	1962	Reds	23	5	.821
Larry Jansen	1947	Giants	21	5	.808
Boo Ferriss	1946	Red Sox	25	6	.806
Juan Marichal	1966	Giants	25	6	.806

3.21 **C. Dean Chance**

Fate helped Chance break Sandy Koufax's monopoly on the Cy
Young award in 1964. Koufax appeared headed for another
Cy Young with a win–loss record of 19–5 in 28 starts and a 1.74
ERA, when he was sidelined with an elbow problem. In Koufax's
absence, the voters selected Chance as the majors' top pitcher in a
landslide. Despite pitching for a mediocre team, the Los Angeles
Angels righthander posted a sparkling 20–9 record with a 1.65
ERA and 11 shutouts, the most whitewashes by an AL pitcher since
Walter Johnson in 1913.

INFIELD CHATTER

More than any other sport, baseball inspires wise and witty sayings. Fittingly, some of the most colourful quips are about the game's best players. Listed below are 16 baseball greats. Your task is to match the player to the quote which describes him. We also supply the author of the quote, which may help make things clearer.

(Answers are on page 138)

Don Drysdale	Pete Rose	Mickey Mantle	Willie Mays
Stan Musial	Bob Gibson	Brooks Robinson	Warren Spahn
Boog Powell	Yogi Berra	Gaylord Perry	Ted Williams
Sandy Koufax	Hank Aaron	Satchel Paige	Joe DiMaggio

1. "I can't very well tell my batters, 'Don't hit it to him.' Wherever they hit it, he's there anyway." —GIL HODGES

2. "Slapping a rattlesnake across the face with the back of your hand is safer than trying to fool _____." —CLAUDE OSTEEN

3. "_____ could have hit .300 with a fountain pen." —JOE GARAGIOLA

4. "He plays the bag like he came down from a higher league." —ED HURLEY, UMPIRE

5. "Trying to hit _____ is like trying to drink coffee with a fork." —WILLIE STARGELL

6. "I don't think _____ will ever get into the Hall of Fame. He'll never stop pitching." —STAN MUSIAL

7. "If _____ held out his right arm, he'd be a railroad crossing." —JOE GARAGIOLA

8. "_____ is the luckiest pitcher I've ever seen. He always picks the night to pitch when the other team doesn't score any runs."
—TIM McCARVER

9. "_____ is a man who was meant to play ball on hot afternoons on the grass of big cities. He never belonged in the rain."
—JIMMY CANNON, SPORTSWRITER

10: "_____ has been approached by every investment firm in San Francisco. After all, he's the man who took a 39-cent jar of Vaseline and made himself into a $100,000 pitcher."
—BOBBY BOLIN

11. "The trick against _____ is to hit him before he hits you."
—ORLANDO CEPEDA

12. "Did they tell me how to pitch to _____ ? Sure they did. It was great advice, very encouraging. They said he had no weakness, won't swing at a bad ball, has the best eyes in the business and can kill you with one swing."
—BOBBY SHANTZ

13. "Everybody who roomed with him said it took five years off their career."
—WHITEY FORD

14. "He threw me his arms, his elbows, his foot and his wrist, everything but the ball. The next thing I knew he threw the ball . . . to my surprise."
—EDDIE YOST

15. "He is what Norman Rockwell would draw for a *Saturday Evening Post* cover if he was doing a ballplayer. _____ looks as if he should have a dog with him."
—JIM MURRAY, SPORTSWRITER

16. "He ain't much to look at, and he looks like he's doing everything wrong, but he can hit. He got a couple of hits off us on wild pitches."
—MEL OTT

Chapter Four

4

FAMOUS FIRSTS

Some baseball firsts are also lasts. On April 25, 1952, Hoyt Wilhelm of the New York Giants homered in his first major league at-bat. Just for good measure he followed with a triple in his next trip to the plate. This was not, however, a sign of things to come. Wilhelm never hit another homer or triple in his 21-year career. Luckily, he had other talents. In 1985, the knuckleball artist became the first relief pitcher to be elected to the Hall of Fame.

(Answers are on page 55)

4.1   In 1953, Al Rosen of the Indians became the first AL player to be elected MVP by a unanimous vote. Who was the first NL player to sweep the MVP voting?

A. Stan Musial in 1948
B. Willie Mays in 1954
C. Sandy Koufax in 1963
D. Orlando Cepeda in 1967

4.2 **Who was the first major leaguer to earn $100,000 a year?**
A. Joe DiMaggio
B. Hank Greenberg
C. Willie Mays
D. Mickey Mantle

4.3 **Jackie Robinson broke the colour barrier in the National League. Who was the American League's first black player?**
A. Larry Doby of the Indians
B. Hank Thompson of the Browns
C. Sam Hairston of the White Sox
D. Elston Howard of the Yankees

4.4 **Several teams changed postal codes during the 1950s. Which relocation occurred first?**
A. The Browns moved from St. Louis to Baltimore
B. The Athletics moved from Philadelphia to Kansas City
C. The Braves moved from Boston to Milwaukee
D. The Dodgers moved from Brooklyn to Los Angeles

4.5 **Who pitched the first no-hitter for an expansion team?**
A. Dick Donovan of the Washington Senators
B. Bo Belinsky of the Los Angeles Angels
C. Don Nottebart of the Houston Colt .45s
D. Al Jackson of the New York Mets

4.6 **The Cy Young award for the best pitcher in the majors was first presented in 1956. Who won the plaque?**
A. Don Newcombe
B. Warren Spahn
C. Early Wynn
D. Whitey Ford

4.7 **In what year did Topps issue its first Mickey Mantle baseball card?**
A. 1950
B. 1951
C. 1952
D. 1953

4.8 **Who was the first player to hit 30 homers in both leagues?**
A. Frank Howard
B. Dick Stuart
C. Roger Maris
D. Frank Robinson

4.9 **Who was the first Latino player to win an MVP award?**
A. Tony Oliva
B. Minnie Minoso
C. Zoilo Versalles
D. Roberto Clemente

4.10 **Who was the first National Leaguer to win back-to-back MVP awards?**
A. Hank Aaron
B. Ernie Banks
C. Willie Mays
D. Roy Campanella

4.11 **Who blanked the New York Mets 6–0 in 1964, to become the first NL pitcher to toss a perfect game since 1880?**
A. Sammy Ellis
B. Jim Bunning
C. Sandy Koufax
D. Ray Sadecki

4.12 **In 1965, who became the first major leaguer to play all nine positions in one game?**
A. Ruben Amaro
B. Tom Tresh
C. Rich Rollins
D. Bert Campaneris

4.13 **Who hit the first home run at Houston's Astrodome?**
A. Rusty Staub
B. Willie McCovey
C. Mickey Mantle
D. Don Drysdale

4.14 **Who managed the Baltimore Orioles to their first world championship in 1966?**
A. Paul Richards
B. Earl Weaver
C. Hank Bauer
D. Billy Hitchcock

4.15 **Which first is false?**
A. Jackie Robinson was the first black player to win a batting title
B. Satchel Paige was the first black player to pitch in a World Series
C. Willie Mays was the first black player to lead his league in home runs
D. Elston Howard was the first black player to win the AL MVP award

4.16 **In 1953, who became the only pitcher in the 20th century to pitch a no-hitter in his first major league start?**
A. Johnny Podres of the Dodgers
B. Joey Jay of the Braves
C. Dick Tomanek of the Indians
D. Bobo Holloman of the Browns

4.17 **Which team featured the majors' first all switch-hitting infield?**
A. The 1950 Philadelphia Phillies
B. The 1958 Baltimore Orioles
C. The 1965 Los Angeles Dodgers
D. The 1966 New York Yankees

4.18 **Who was hired as the first manager of the New York Mets on October 2, 1962?**
A. Gil Hodges
B. Casey Stengel
C. Branch Rickey
D. Wes Westrum

Answers

FAMOUS FIRSTS

4.1   **D. Orlando Cepeda in 1967**

Cepeda's unanimous selection, the first in the National League since they began handing out MVP awards in both leagues in 1931, is somewhat surprising, as his stats (.325 batting average, 25 homers, 111 RBI) were less than phenomenal. But Cepeda did play a major role in leading the St. Louis Cardinals to the NL pennant.

4.2   **B. Hank Greenberg**

Greenberg reached the six-figure mark in 1947, three years before DiMaggio. Mays and Mantle would not be paid $100,000 a year until 1963. A salary dispute caused the veteran Detroit Tigers star to be released on waivers in 1947, a surprising move considering Greenberg had led the American League in homers and RBI in 1946. The 36-year-old slugger was quickly claimed by the Pittsburgh Pirates. Initially, Greenberg considered retiring, but he was dissuaded when the Pirates offered him a contract worth more than $100,000, plus a racehorse. To help out his power stroke, the Pirates created an enclosure in front of the left-field wall, which shortened the distance to the fence by 30 feet. The area was promptly christened "Greenberg Gardens." It wasn't Greenberg, but teammate Ralph Kiner, who profited most from the renovation. Kiner blasted 51 homers. Greenberg hit .248 with 25 homers and 74 RBI and retired at the season's end.

4.3   **A. Larry Doby of the Indians**

Bill Veeck, owner of the Cleveland Indians, began the integration process in the American League by acquiring 23-year-old outfielder Larry Doby from the Newark Eagles of the Negro Leagues. Doby played his first game with the Indians on July 5, 1947, just 12 days before another black player, Hank Thompson, made his debut with the St. Louis Browns.

4.4   **C. The Braves moved from Boston to Milwaukee**
Tired of consistently drawing fewer fans than his crosstown rivals, the Boston Red Sox, owner Lou Perini moved the Braves to Milwaukee in March 1953. It was the first franchise shift in the majors since 1902 and everyone was curious to observe the outcome. The results were astounding. The Braves' attendance jumped from 281,278 to a major league record 1,826,397, then cleared the two-million mark for the next four years. By 1958, the Browns, Athletics, Dodgers and Giants had all followed the Braves' example and relocated.

ATTENDANCE OF RELOCATED TEAMS

Old City	Final Year	New City	First Year
Boston	281,278	Milwaukee	1,826,397
St. Louis	297,238	Baltimore	1,060,910
Philadelphia	304,666	Kansas City	1,393,054
Brooklyn	1,028,250	Los Angeles	1,845,556
New York	653,923	San Francisco	1,272,625

4.5   **B. Bo Belinsky of the Los Angeles Angels**
The pool-hustling playboy pitched his gem against the Baltimore Orioles on May 5, 1962, after partying until 4:00 A.M. with a woman he had just met. The no-hitter gave him a 5–0 record in his rookie season, but his career went downhill from that point on. According to John Thorn and John Holway in their book *The Pitcher*, Belinsky blamed his decline on the fact he never found the woman again. "She was my good luck charm. When I lost her, I lost my pitching luck." Belinsky also complained that he did not make money off his no-hitter. In fact, he said it cost him money. "I had to buy drinks for everyone. It was like a hole-in-one."

4.6   A. Don Newcombe

The Dodger fireballer not only won the inaugural Cy Young award in 1956, he captured the NL MVP award as well. Newcombe was 27–7, with an ERA of 3.06, and held opposing hitters to a league-low .221 batting average, as he led Brooklyn to the pennant. Unfortunately for the Dodgers, Newk came up empty in the World Series. The Yankees blitzed the Dodger ace in his two starts, saddling him with a 21.21 ERA, en route to winning the Series in seven games.

4.7   C. 1952

Topps' 1952 Mickey Mantle card is the most famous and most valuable baseball card issued since World War II. In mint condition this tiny piece of cardboard fetches $40,000. Though it is not Mantle's true rookie card (Bowman produced a Mantle card in 1951), it is his most prized because it appeared in the first full-scale baseball card set issued by Topps, the Brooklyn chewing gum company that dominated the sports card industry in the 1950s and 1960s. Mantle's impact on card collecting, and on Topps in particular, was so profound that after Mantle's death in 1995, in tribute to his memory, the company officially retired the number seven from all its future baseball sets.

4.8   B. Dick Stuart

The sideburned slugger clubbed 35 homers for the Pittsburgh Pirates in 1961, but when he slumped to just 16 round-trippers in 1962, the Pirates traded Stuart and pitcher Jack Lamabe to the Boston Red Sox for catcher Don Pagliaroni and pitcher Don Schwall. Stuart found Fenway Park to his liking. He collected a career-high 42 homers and 118 RBI for Boston in 1963, to become the first player to hit 30 homers in both leagues.

4.9   C. Zoilo Versalles

Contrary to what one might expect, Roberto Clemente was not the first Latino player to capture an MVP award. The classy Puerto Rican first won the award in 1966, one year after the Cuban-born Versalles was voted MVP in the American League. Versalles was a sparkplug on the 1965 pennant-winning Minnesota Twins. Hitting with surprising power for his size, the 146-pound shortstop paced the AL in doubles (45), triples (12), runs scored (126) and total bases (308), and won a Gold Glove for his stellar fielding.

4.10   B. Ernie Banks

Banks is fondly remembered for his sunny disposition and his famous expression, "It's a lovely day for baseball. Let's play two!" Yet in the 1950s, the Cubs shortstop wielded one of the most lethal bats in the majors. In 1958, Banks banged out a league-leading 47 homers, collected 129 RBI and batted .313 to defeat Willie Mays and Hank Aaron in the MVP voting. In 1959, he clubbed 45 homers, 143 RBI and had a .304 average to outpoll Eddie Mathews and Aaron. His back-to-back MVP awards are noteworthy, not only because of the high calibre of players he had to beat, but also because the Cubs finished under .500 in both years.

4.11   B. Jim Bunning

Bunning's perfect game for the Phillies, the first in the NL since 1880, came on Father's Day in 1964. It was Bunning's second no-hitter; he tossed his first in 1958 with the Detroit Tigers. An under-rated pitcher, who had the misfortune of playing on a lot of mediocre teams, Bunning ranked second on the all-time strikeout list behind Walter Johnson when he retired after the 1971 season.

4.12   D. Bert Campaneris

Campaneris was a versatile player, but the only reason he played all nine positions in a game was because Kansas City Athletics owner Charlie Finley wanted to make headlines. The event occurred on September 9, 1965, against the Los Angeles Angels. Only one other player has since duplicated the feat: Cesar Tovar of the Minnesota Twins in a game versus Finley's Oakland Athletics in 1968. Ironically, the first batter Tovar faced in his one-inning pitching stint was Bert Campaneris.

4.13   C. Mickey Mantle

Billed as "the eighth wonder of the world," the Astrodome hosted its first baseball game on April 9, 1965, an exhibition contest between the Houston Astros and the New York Yankees. Texas

Governor John Connally threw out the first pitch and Mantle hit the first space shot in the Dome, launching a blast over the centre-field fence to break a scoreless tie in the sixth inning. Houston eventually won the game 2–1 to send the Texas fans home happy, but it was an Oklahoman from the American League who hit the first homer.

4.14 C. Hank Bauer

Bauer piloted the Orioles to the AL pennant and a World Series championship in his third season at the helm of the team, aided in great part by an off-season trade that brought Triple Crown-winner Frank Robinson over from Cincinnati. The Birds failed to repeat in 1967 and Bauer was eventually replaced by Earl Weaver midway through the 1968 season.

4.15 C. Willie Mays was the first black player to lead his league in home runs

Larry Doby of the Cleveland Indians twice led the American League in home runs (1952 and 1954), before Mays first topped the National League in four-baggers in 1955. All of the other statements are true. Jackie Robinson of the Dodgers became the first black player to win a batting title when he led the NL in 1949; Satchel Paige became the first black player to pitch in a World Series when he tossed two-thirds of an inning for the Indians in 1948; and Elston Howard became the first black player to capture the AL MVP award with the Yankees in 1963.

4.16 D. Bobo Holloman of the Browns

Only two pitchers in St. Louis Browns history have ever pitched a no-no and both were named Bobo. The odds against this happening are high enough on their own, but when you consider that the second Bobo did it in his first major league start, the probabilities become astronomical. Bobo Newsom, who turned the trick in 1934, was a legitimate big leaguer who won 211 games during his career, but Bobo Holloman qualifies as the worst pitcher to manage the feat. The 27-year-old rookie reliever, who was blessed with more confidence than ability, had been pestering manager Marty

Marion for a starting assignment since the start of the 1953 season. Marion intended to send Holloman down to the minors but decided to give him one courtesy appearance before shipping him out. With the aid of several incredible fielding plays, Holloman responded by tossing a no-hitter against the Athletics. He remained in the starting rotation for two more months, but never completed another game. By the end of July, Holloman had a 3–7 record and a 5.26 ERA, and the Browns sent him to the minors. He never appeared in the majors again.

4.17 C. The 1965 Los Angeles Dodgers

The majors' first all-switch hitting infield was composed of Wes Parker at first base, Jim Lefebvre at second, Jim Gilliam at third and Maury Wills at shortstop. The unit remained together until the end of 1966, when Gilliam retired and Wills was traded.

4.18 B. Casey Stengel

Stengel opened his first press conference as the manager of the expansion New York Mets by stating, "It's a great honour for me to be joining the Knickerbockers." Stengel had the wrong sport, but he was the right man for the job. The Old Professor's scrambled syntax and warped wit helped sell a team that was better at beating itself than anyone else in the National League. "Come and see my amazin' Mets," Stengel told reporters. "I've been in this game a hundred years, but I'm learning new ways to lose I never knew existed before."

S T R I K E   ' E M   O U T

Each of the horizontal rows in the box below contains the last names of players from the glory years. The letters of their names appear in normal order from left to right, but in each row some extra letters have been added. Your job is to "strike out" the players one by one. Once you've crossed out all their names, the remaining letters, reading down, column by column, from left to right, will reveal what these players have in common. *(Answers are on page 138)*

T	O	L	L	A	I	T	V	C	A
F	U	W	R	I	E	L	L	R	O
H	R	U	L	N	N	E	T	L	S
K	Y	A	L	G	I	N	I	E	W
F	A	O	I	N	M	A	N	Y	S
D	A	A	E	V	B	I	S	O	N
A	L	S	H	B	A	U	R	N	S
E	M	N	A	U	N	T	G	L	E

Chapter Five

WHO AM I?

When Topps Chewing Gum Inc. began issuing baseball cards in the 1950s, it sent scouts to minor league camps to sign exclusive contracts with anyone the company regarded as a major league prospect. In 1958, a Topps agent chose not to sign one player because he felt there was no way he would ever make it to the majors. The player later became a star in the big leagues and even won an MVP award, but because of the snub he refused to sign with Topps until 1967. Who was the one that got away?

In this chapter we alter the multiple-choice format and supply all 18 answers. Match the players listed below with their Who am I? descriptions. The remaining 19th name is our mystery man.

(Answers are on page 66)

Joe Adcock	Nellie Fox	Bo Belinsky	Jackie Jensen
Sal Maglie	Jim Maloney	Frank Howard	Luis Aparicio
Ryne Duren	Vada Pinson	Bob Turley	Harmon Killebrew
Dick Groat	Stu Miller	Richie Allen	Carroll Hardy
Maury Wills	Gene Conley	Mickey Lolich	

5.1   I led my league in stolen bases a record nine times in a row.
Who am I?

5.2   I hit 10 homers in a six-game period in 1968, the same year I led
the American League in circuit blasts. **Who am I?**

5.3   I drilled 205 hits, including a league-high 47 doubles, scored 131
runs and batted .316 in my first full season in 1959, but I was
not voted Rookie of the Year because I had lost my eligibility by
batting six too many times in 1958. **Who am I?**

5.4   Rumour had it I was legally blind, which, combined with my
blazing fastball, made hitters think twice about digging in at the
plate. But poor eyesight didn't stop me from becoming the
bullpen ace of the New York Yankees in the late 1950s. **Who am I?**

5.5   I belted more than 40 homers eight times in my career, but I only
hit a grand total of 24 triples in 8,147 at-bats, which tells you
something about my foot speed. **Who am I?**

5.6   After being picked up on waivers from the Cleveland Indians
in 1956, I won 13 games down the stretch, including a no-hitter
versus the Phillies, to help the Dodgers take the NL pennant.
Who am I?

5.7   I pitched 16 years in the majors, posted 105 wins, 154 saves and
won an ERA crown, but I am best remembered for literally being
blown off the mound during the 1961 All-Star game at Candlestick
Park. **Who am I?**

5.8   I was no magician with the glove, but I more than made up for
it with my offense. In my first season I set a new league record for
total bases by a rookie. **Who am I?**

5.9   A former MVP winner, I was at the midway point of a brilliant
career when I quit the game in 1962, because I couldn't overcome
my fear of flying. **Who am I?**

5.10   Although I once tossed a no-hitter, I was more famous for my off-field activities than anything I did on the diamond. During my career I dated Ann-Margret, Tina Louise, Connie Stevens and Mamie Van Doren. **Who am I?**

5.11   I was the first AL hurler to win a Cy Young award, and at last count, I am still the only Baltimore Orioles pitcher to lead the AL in strikeouts. **Who am I?**

5.12   You could count on me to make contact. I led my league in fewest strikeouts 11 times. In fact, during my entire career I never fanned more than 18 times in a season. **Who am I?**

5.13   I am the only All-American college basketball player to win an MVP award in the major leagues. **Who am I?**

5.14   I am the only player to ever pinch-hit for Ted Williams. I also pinch-hit for Roger Maris and Carl Yastrzemski. Those are impressive credentials, but with a lifetime batting average of .225 and a paltry 17 career homers, only trivia buffs remember my name. **Who am I?**

5.15   In a game at Ebbets Field in 1954, I slugged four homers and a double, giving me 18 total bases, a one-game record. **Who am I?**

5.16   I hit the only homer of my career in a World Series game. That's a feat no other player can lay claim to. Of course, few other players ever won three games in one Series, which is another item on my resume. **Who am I?**

5.17   I was a man for all seasons. I won a world championship with the Milwaukee Braves in 1957 and won three championships with the Boston Celtics in the NBA. **Who am I?**

5.18   I whiffed more than 200 batters four straight years during the 1960s. In 1965, I became the first pitcher in history to toss two extra-inning no-hitters in a season. **Who am I?**

Answers

W H O   A M   I ?

5.1   Several years before Maury Wills kick-started the stolen base revo-
lution in the National League, **Luis Aparicio** was already giving
pitchers fits in the junior circuit. The little shortstop led the American League in stolen bases a record nine years in a row from 1956
to 1964, before finally relinquishing his king-of-thieves crown to
Bert Campaneris.

5.2   Hulking six-foot-eight, 275-pound **Frank Howard** was dubbed
"the Capital Punisher" during his years with the Washington Senators from 1965 to 1971. As one might expect from his Bunyanesque
dimensions, Howard's forte was hitting the long ball. In a six-game
span in May 1968, the giant outfielder exhibited an awesome display of muscle power, blasting a record 10 homers in just 20 at-bats.

5.3   **Vada Pinson** not only had a great baseball name, the whippet-lean
outfielder was also an electrifying talent. Combined with Frank
Robinson, he gave the Cincinnati Reds a deadly one-two punch at
the heart of their batting order in the late 1950s and early 1960s.
But despite topping the 200-hit mark four times and amassing
2,757 hits in his career, Pinson was perpetually overshadowed by
the other great outfielders of his era. Like those six extra at-bats
that cost him the Rookie-of-the-Year award, Pinson's fate was to
fall just short of true greatness.

5.4   **Ryne Duren** was a terrifying figure on the mound, not just because
his fastball was clocked in the high nineties, but because he
seemed only vaguely familiar with the location of the plate. Duren

wore tinted, Coke-bottle-thick glasses and used to routinely fire a few warmup pitches over the catcher's head and into the screen behind home plate. It wasn't all an act. Duren was wild (he once hit the on-deck batter with an errant pitch), but his wildness probably helped more than it hurt him by making hitters edgy. Booze eventually curtailed Duren's velocity and his career, but for a few years in the late 1950s he was the AL's dominant reliever and a real conversation piece. As Casey Stengel noted, "Whenever he came into the game people would stop eating their popcorn."

5.5 **Harmon Killebrew** was always looking to hit one out and with his power, there was a good chance the Idaho strongboy would succeed. Of Killebrew's 2,086 career hits, 573 (27 per cent) were homers. He led the AL in four-baggers six times. But hitting triples was another matter entirely. Only once in 22 years did Killebrew collect more than two. He simply had no speed. Even making it to second was a struggle. His high for doubles was 27 in 1966.

5.6 During his years with the New York Giants in the early 1950s, **Sal Maglie**'s competitive fire and his knack for beating Brooklyn in big games made him public enemy number one at Ebbets Field. So it was a big surprise when the Dodgers plucked the 39-year-old veteran from the waiver list in May 1956 and put him into the club's starting rotation. The gamble paid off handsomely as Maglie went 13–5 the rest of the way to help Brooklyn edge the Milwaukee Braves for the pennant by one game.

5.7 Candlestick Park was known as "the Cave of the Winds," and a national television audience discovered why at the All-Star game on July 11, 1961. In the ninth inning, with AL runners on first and second and the NL All-Stars clinging to a 3–2 lead, pitcher **Stu Miller** entered the game in relief. As Miller went into his motion and prepared to pitch to Rocky Colavito, a vicious gust picked him up and literally blew the 165-pound hurler off the pitching rubber. Ignoring Miller's objections, umpire Stan Landes called a balk. Miller overcame the setback and eventually got the win in the game, but nothing he ever did in his career rivalled the notoriety he received for getting blown off the mound.

5.8 Rookie **Richie Allen** made an alarming 41 errors at third base in 1964, but his booming bat was a big reason why the Philadelphia Phillies contended for the NL pennant. Allen batted .318, scored a league-leading 125 runs and hit 29 homers with 91 RBI. His 352 total bases topped the league and established a new record for NL freshmen.

5.9 A fear of flying caused **Jackie Jensen** to retire twice, in 1960, and then again in 1962, the second time for good. The phobia cut short an impressive career. In a six-year span from 1954 to 1959, the Boston Red Sox outfielder drove in 667 runs, more than anyone else in the American League. In 1958, Jensen hit 35 homers, drove in 122 runs and won the AL MVP award, despite playing for a third-place team.

5.10 Ironically, when **Bo Belinsky** finally made the majors it was with a team that had a halo on its cap. After joining the Los Angeles Angels in 1962, the cocky southpaw quickly gained a reputation as serious carouser. He spent more time cruising around town in his candy-apple-red convertible than he ever did preparing for games. As his one-time roommate Albie Pearson noted: "I was just Bo's answering service. I never saw him at night. I just roomed with his suitcase." Belinsky became a fixture at Hollywood parties and dated numerous starlets, including the Shah of Iran's former wife, Queen Soraya. For a time he was engaged to blonde bombshell Mamie Van Doren. When they broke up, Belinsky quipped, "I needed her like Custer needed Indians."

5.11 "Bullet" **Bob Turley** spent only one year in a Baltimore Orioles uniform, but that season (1954) he led the American League in strikeouts with 185 Ks, something no Oriole moundsman has managed to duplicate. His performance caught the attention of the New York Yankees who acquired the hard-thowing righty in a trade in 1955. Turley had his best season with the Bronx Bombers in 1958, when he went 21–7 and won the Cy Young. Turley continued his heroics in the 1958 World Series, winning game five, saving game six and winning game seven in relief, as the Yankees rallied from a 3–1 deficit in games to defeat the Milwaukee Braves.

5.12   Few players were better at getting wood on the ball than **Nellie Fox**. Choking up on his thick-handled bat, the slap-hitting, tobacco-chewing Fox was one tough out. He led the American League in fewest strikeouts 10 times with the Chicago White Sox and he led the National League once in the category with the Houston Colt .45s. Fox's remarkable total of only 216 strikeouts in 9,232 career at-bats is the third-best ratio in major league history.

THE HARDEST BATTERS TO STRIKE OUT*

Player	Yrs Active	ABs	Ks	AB/K Ratio
Joe Sewell	1920–33	7,132	114	63 to 1
Lloyd Waner	1927–45	7,732	173	45 to 1
Nellie Fox	1947–65	9,232	216	43 to 1
Tommy Holmes	1942–52	4,992	122	41 to 1

* Players who played before 1913 are not included in the chart because no strikeout stats are available for those years.

5.13   **Dick Groat** was an All-American basketball star at Duke University and played for a short time in the NBA after he joined the Pittsburgh Pirates in 1952. In 1960, the hard-nosed shortstop hit .325 to lead the National League in batting average and won the MVP award. Groat capped off his career season when the Bucs won the World Series in a seven-game thriller against the New York Yankees.

5.14   There is no logical reason why a guy with a .225 lifetime average would be called upon to pinch-hit for three of the game's greatest hitters, but it happened nonetheless. **Carroll Hardy** pinch-hit for Roger Maris with the Cleveland Indians in 1958, and promptly clouted his first big league homer, a three-run shot to win the game. In 1960, with the Red Sox, Hardy earned the distinction of being the only player to ever pinch-hit for Ted Williams. He got the nod on that occasion after Williams fouled a ball off his foot and had to leave the game. In 1961, Hardy completed his rare trifecta when manager Pinky Higgins sent him into a game to swing the bat in place of rookie Carl Yastrzemski.

5.15 On July 31, 1954, at Ebbets Field, **Joe Adcock** of the Milwaukee Braves came to the plate five times, was thrown seven pitches and hit four homers and a double. It was a devastating display of power and the embarrassed Dodger pitchers didn't let it go unpunished. The next day, Clem Labine beaned Adcock. Six weeks later, a Don Newcombe fastball smashed Adcock's right hand and sidelined him for the rest of the season.

5.16 In 16 seasons and 840 career at-bats, **Mickey Lolich** stroked only one homer, but it came at an opportune time—in the third inning of a tight game in the 1968 World Series. The blow and Lolich's stellar pitching helped the Detroit Tigers even the Series at one game apiece with the St. Louis Cardinals. Lolich proved to be the Redbirds' nemesis, winning three games in the Series, including the crucial seventh game in a dramatic duel with Bob Gibson.

5.17 Basketball-playing pitcher **Gene Conley** had a knack for playing with winners. He was with the Milwaukee Braves when they took the World Series in 1957, and he was a member of the NBA champion Boston Celtics in 1959, 1960 and 1961. Conley spent the last three years of his baseball career in Boston with the Red Sox, where the unfamiliar sensation of losing eventually got to him. In New York, in 1962, after a humiliating loss to the Yankees, Conley walked off the team bus in the middle of a traffic jam and disappeared. The six-foot-eight hurler was next spotted three days later, in a line at the airport attempting to board a plane to Israel—with no luggage, no passport and in an advanced state of inebriation. His motivation is open to speculation.

5.18 Only seven times in the majors have pitchers carried no-hitters into extra innings and flame-throwing **Jim Maloney** of the Cincinnati Reds accounted for two of them, both in 1965. Maloney lost the first of his masterpieces 1–0, on June 14, when he gave up a homer to the Mets in the 11th. On August 19, teammate Leo Cardenas hit a homer in the top of the 10th to break a scoreless duel with the Cubs and Maloney held Chicago hitless in the bottom of the frame to get the win and the no-no.

ALL–STAR NUMBERS

Pitcher Don Drysdale owns the unique distinction of starting two All-Star games in one year. How is this possible? From 1957 to 1962, two All-Star games were contested each season, several weeks apart. Drysdale was given both starting assignments for the National League in 1959.

   Listed below are the uniform numbers of the starting nine from two All-Star teams, one from the NL and one from the AL. See if you can match the players with the numbers that their teams retired in their honour.   *(Answers are on page 138)*

NATIONAL LEAGUE

6   9   14   21   24   32   39   41   44

_____ Left field: Hank Aaron (Braves)

_____ Centre field: Willie Mays (Giants)

_____ Right field: Roberto Clemente (Pirates)

_____ Third base: Eddie Mathews (Braves)

_____ Shortstop: Ernie Banks (Cubs)

_____ Second base: Bill Mazeroski (Pirates)

_____ First base: Stan Musial (Cardinals)

_____ Catcher: Roy Campanella (Dodgers)

_____ Pitcher: Sandy Koufax (Dodgers)

GAME 5

AMERICAN LEAGUE

2   3   5   7   8   9   11   16   20

_____ Left field: Ted Williams (Red Sox)

_____ Centre field: Mickey Mantle (Yankees)

_____ Right field: Frank Robinson (Orioles)

_____ Third base: Brooks Robinson (Orioles)

_____ Shortstop: Luis Aparicio (White Sox)

_____ Second base: Nellie Fox (White Sox)

_____ First base: Harmon Killebrew (Twins)

_____ Catcher: Yogi Berra (Yankees)

_____ Pitcher: Whitey Ford (Yankees)

Chapter Six

TEAMS, TOWNS AND TRADITIONS

We will never see another dynasty like the one established by the post-World War II New York Yankees. The Bronx Bombers claimed the American League pennant an incredible 14 times in 16 years from 1949 to 1964. In fact, if not for Al Lopez, the Yanks might have made it 16 straight. The only teams to interrupt their stay in the AL penthouse were the 1954 Cleveland Indians and the 1959 Chicago White Sox, and both clubs were managed by Lopez. *(Answers are on page 79)*

(Answers are on page 79)

6.1 **"Open the window, Aunt Minnie, here it comes!" was the famous line used by broadcaster Rosey Rowsell to signal a home run. For which team did Rowsell handle the play-by-play?**

A. The Brooklyn Dodgers
B. The Chicago White Sox
C. The Pittsburgh Pirates
D. The St. Louis Cardinals

6.2　Which club hired a hypnotist in 1950 in an effort to rid its
players of a defeatist complex?
A. The Chicago Cubs
B. The Pittsburgh Pirates
C. The Washington Senators
D. The St. Louis Browns

6.3　From which team did the Yankees acquire Roger Maris?
A. The Boston Red Sox
B. The Cleveland Indians
C. The Milwaukee Braves
D. The Kansas City Athletics

6.4　Which 1960s club posted a woeful team batting average of .214,
the lowest in the majors since the dead-ball era?
A. The 1965 New York Mets
B. The 1967 Chicago White Sox
C. The 1967 Washington Senators
D. The 1968 New York Yankees

6.5　In 1954, the International League expanded outside North
America and granted a franchise to which city?
A. Managua, Nicaragua
B. Havana, Cuba
C. Caracas, Venezuela
D. Santo Domingo, Dominican Republic

6.6　Which team chose to dispense with a manager in 1961 and 1962,
experimenting instead with a revolving staff of coaches?
A. The Cleveland Indians
B. The Baltimore Orioles
C. The Chicago Cubs
D. The St. Louis Cardinals

6.7　Which team changed its name during the 1950s for political
reasons?
A. The Boston Braves
B. The St. Louis Browns

C. The Cincinnati Reds

D. The Washington Senators

6.8 **Prior to the 1951 season, Connie Mack stepped down as the manager of the Philadelphia Athletics. How old was Mack?**
A. 58
B. 68
C. 78
D. 88

6.9 **Which team unveiled a plan to build a domed stadium with a retractable roof and a synthetic playing surface in 1952?**
A. The Pittsburgh Pirates
B. The Washington Senators
C. The Cleveland Indians
D. The Brooklyn Dodgers

6.10 **What was the name of the tiny, 22,000-seat ballpark that the expansion Los Angeles Angels called home in their first season in 1961?**
A. Stadler Stadium
B. Gilmore Field
C. Wrigley Field
D. Hollywood Park

6.11 **Which defunct ballpark was famous for its 250-foot homers and 450-foot fly outs?**
A. Forbes Field
B. Ebbets Field
C. The Polo Grounds
D. Sportsman's Park

6.12 **A dispute over harmonica playing proved to be a turning point for the fortunes of which team?**
A. The 1954 New York Giants
B. The 1957 Milwaukee Braves
C. The 1964 New York Yankees
D. The 1967 Boston Red Sox

6.13 The Boston Red Sox was the last major league club to put a black player in its lineup. In what year did the Red Sox finally integrate?
A. 1953
B. 1955
C. 1957
D. 1959

6.14 Which team produced the most batting champions between 1946 and 1968?
A. The Pittsburgh Pirates
B. The St. Louis Cardinals
C. The Boston Red Sox
D. The New York Yankees

6.15 In 1960, which two teams completed the only managerial swap in major league history, as Jimmy Dykes and Joe Gordon changed uniforms?
A. Cleveland and Detroit
B. Baltimore and Kansas City
C. Philadelphia and St. Louis
D. San Francisco and Cincinnati

6.16 Which owner tried to give his club a home-field advantage by changing the distance from home plate to the outfield fences from game to game?
A. Lou Perini of the Braves
B. Charlie Finley of the Athletics
C. Bill Veeck of the Indians
D. Clark Griffith of the Senators

6.17 The New York Mets finshed in last place in their inaugural season in 1962. How many games did the Mets finish out of first?
A. 30
B. 40
C. 50
D. 60

Answers

TEAMS, TOWNS AND TRADITIONS

6.1 **C. The Pittsburgh Pirates**

The voice of the Pirates in the late 1940s and 1950s, Rowsell invented his own expressions to describe the play of his beloved Buccos. A Pirates' extra-base hit was a "doozie maroney," a strike-out was a "dipsy doodle," and the bases were never loaded, they were "FOB"(full of Bucs). But Rowsell is best remembered for his novel method of signalling Pirate home runs. The announcer invented a fictitious character named Aunt Minnie, who suppos-edly lived in an apartment with a window facing Forbes Field. Whenever it looked like a ball was headed in her direction, he'd shout his trademark line and smash a light bulb near the micro-phone to produce the desired sound effect.

6.2 **D. The St. Louis Browns**

The Browns were consistently awful in the late 1940s, finishing between 37 and 44 games out of first from 1946 to 1949. In a bid to improve the club in 1950, owners Bill and Charlie Dewitt announced they would employ the services of a psychologist and hypnotist named David Tracy to boost the confidence of the Browns players by autosuggestion. Manager Zack Taylor consid-ered the idea idiotic. Fearing Tracy might put the players to sleep on the diamond, he banned him from the dugout. Sportswriters had a field day. After hearing that the doctor would try to help Brownie pitchers "keep the ball away from Joe DiMaggio," Bob Cooke ruefully noted that was no problem. "Sometimes," he wrote, "they keep it 400 feet away from him." With Tracy's sublim-inal assistance, the Browns finished 40 games out of first.

6.3 D. The Kansas City Athletics

The 1959 off-season trade that brought Roger Maris to New York was typical of Yankee–Athletic transactions during the late 1950s—extremely one-sided. Repeatedly, the also-ran A's sent the Yanks promising young talent or stretch-run help for unproven performers or washed-up discards. Clete Boyer, Bobby Shantz, Ralph Terry, Enos Slaughter, Ryne Duren, Hector Lopez and Art Ditmar all came to New York via the K.C. pipeline. Some of the deals were so scandalous, there were suspicions that Yankee owners Dan Topping and Del Webb had some sort of business leverage on Athletics owner Arnold Johnson. To acquire Maris, the Yanks gave up 37-year-old Hank Bauer, sore-armed Don Larsen and second-stringers Norm Siebern and Marv Throneberry.

6.4 D. The 1968 New York Yankees

Batting averages plummeted around the American League in 1968. Carl Yastrzemski was the circuit's only .300 hitter, and just barely, as he hit .301. But it was the once-mighty Yankees who led the way in hitting ineptitude. The club's .214 batting average was the third-worst in major league annals, just ahead of two teams from the dead-ball era: the 1910 Chicago White Sox (.211) and the 1908 Brooklyn Dodgers (.213.).

6.5 B. Havana, Cuba

The Havana Sugar Kings joined the International League in 1954. The franchise was an instant success, drawing 300,000 fans, the second-highest attendance total in the league. The Sugar Kings had their best year in 1959, when they defeated Minneapolis to win the Junior World Series. But political tensions between the U.S. and Fidel Castro's communist regime, which assumed power in 1959, spelled doom for Cuba's involvement in Triple A baseball. Midway through the 1960 season, the Havana franchise was transferred to Jersey City.

6.6 C. The Chicago Cubs

In 1961, Phil Wrigley, owner of the lowly Chicago Cubs, created a system of revolving managers. As Wrigley explained: "We certainly cannot do much worse trying a new system than we have done for many years under the old." The original "council of coaches" included Charlie Grimm, Vedie Himsl, Harry Craft, Rip Collins, Elvin Tappe, Lou Klein, Bobby Adams and Rube Walker. The two-year experiment was a colossal flop. Chaos reigned. Each time a new manager took over he introduced a different style of play and penned a different lineup. The only constant was the end result—the Cubs kept losing, finishing second-last in both years.

6.7   C. The Cincinnati Reds
Preposterous as it sounds today, Cincinnati's management changed the club's nickname to the Redlegs during the communist hysteria of the 1950s, to avoid any hint of a connection with the godless forces of evil.

6.8   D. 88
In 1951, at age 88, "The Tall Tactitian" finally stepped down after a mind-boggling 50 years as the Athletics' field boss. Incredibly, Mack began his managing career with the Pittsburgh Pirates in 1894, a year before Babe Ruth was born. In his last season at the helm, Mack was drifting in and out of senility. "I don't even think he knew my name," said Bobby Shantz, one of the A's starting pitchers in 1950.

6.9   D. The Brooklyn Dodgers
It was Ebbets Field's puny seating capacity of 32,000 and not a deterioration in the facilities that caused Dodger owner Walter O'Malley to begin plotting his escape from Brooklyn. Before he did, however, O'Malley tried to interest the city in the construction of a new ballpark. In 1952, he had an architect draw up plans for a new stadium featuring a retractable roof, heated seats, automatic hot dog vending machines, a synthetic playing surface and a vast shopping centre beneath the stands. But the proposal fell on deaf ears. In 1957, Robert Moses, New York's commissioner in charge of parks, highways and urban projects, told O'Malley, "If I let you build your domed stadium, your ballgames will create a China Wall of traffic in Brooklyn. No one will be able to pass." Moses suggested the Dodgers relocate to Queens. A year later they did move—to Los Angeles.

6.10   C. Wrigley Field

There were two Wrigley Fields, one in Chicago and one in Los Angeles. Both were named after chewing-gum magnate William Wrigley, though the West Coast stadium, which opened in 1925 and served as the home of the Los Angeles Angels of the Pacific Coast League until 1957, was actually the first to bear the name. Its more famous namesake was still called Cubs Park at the time and was not renamed Wrigley Field until 1926. When the PCL Angels moved to Spokane, Washington, in 1958, Wrigley Field West stood empty until Gene Autry's American League expansion team—the reincarnated Los Angeles Angels—took up residence there in 1961. Because the fences in the outfield power alleys extended only a couple of feet farther from home plate than the distance down the foul lines, the stadium was a haven for home run hitters. The Angels and their opponents combined to hammer a major league record 248 round-trippers at Wrigley in 1961, but it was the park's last hurrah. The club moved to Chavez Ravine the next season, which it shared with the Dodgers for four years, before finally moving to Anaheim in 1966 and changing its name to the California Angels.

6.11   C. The Polo Grounds

The home of the New York Giants from 1891 to 1957, and of the New York Mets in 1962 and 1963, the Polo Grounds had one of the oddest configurations of any ballpark. It was shaped like a bathtub with the foul lines extending only 257 feet from the plate in right and 279 in left. The centre-field bleachers, however, were an astounding 460 feet away. Many towering drives that would have been homers in other ballparks were caught by outfielders roaming the vast reaches of centre. The most famous example was Willie Mays's running catch of a 440-foot blast in the first game of the 1954 World Series.

6.12   C. The 1964 New York Yankees

After being swept in a four-game series by the Chicago White Sox, in August 1964, the third-place Yankees looked ready to drop out of the American League pennant race. Rookie manager Yogi Berra had seemingly lost control of his veteran club and morale was low. Riding to the airport from Comiskey Park, a gloomy silence enveloped the team bus. To break the mood, utility infielder Phil Linz began playing "Mary Had a Little Lamb" on his harmonica. Berra turned around in his seat and told Linz to knock it off. "What did Yogi say?" asked Linz. Mickey Mantle leaned over and told him, "He said play it louder." So, Linz kept playing. An irate Berra jumped to his feet, stormed down the aisle and slapped the harmonica out of Linz's hands. He informed the bewildered infielder that he would be fined $250. It was the first time Berra had asserted his authority all season and the team subsequently rallied to win the pennant. As a result of the incident, which received wide coverage in the New York media, Linz landed a $5,000 endorsement deal from the Hoehner Harmonica company and earned a permanent place in Yankee lore.

6.13   D. 1959

On July 21, 1959, more than 12 full years after Jackie Robinson broke the colour barrier, the Boston Red Sox finally changed the all-white complexion of its club by inserting a black player into the lineup—Elijah "Pumpsie" Green, who entered the game as a pinch-runner. Green played 50 games with the Red Sox in 1959, most of them at second base, hitting a meagre .233.

6.14   C. The Boston Red Sox

Although the Red Sox only captured two pennants from 1946–1968, Boston players won 10 league batting titles, easily the most of any team during the era.

TEAMS WITH THE MOST BATTING CHAMPIONS (1946–68)

Titles	Team	Batting Champs
10	Red Sox	T. Williams (4), C. Yastrzemski (3), P. Runnels (2), B. Goodman (1)
6	Cardinals	S. Musial (6)
6	Pirates	R. Clemente (4), D. Groat (1), M. Alou (1)
4	Dodgers	T. Davis (2), J. Robinson (1), C. Furillo (1)
4	Tigers	G. Kell (1), A. Kaline (1), H. Kuenn (1), N. Cash (1)

6.15 **A. Cleveland and Detroit**

In one of baseball's more unusual deals, the Indians and Tigers swapped managers midway through the 1960 campaign. Joe Gordon went to Detroit and Jimmy Dykes came to Cleveland. Neither team improved after the skipper switch. Detroit fired Gordon at the season's end, while Dykes managed one more year in Cleveland before retiring.

6.16 **C. Bill Veeck of the Indians**

Veeck was known for his outrageous publicity stunts, however this manouevre wasn't designed to attract headlines, but rather to give his team an extra edge. In 1948, Veeck had the outfield fences at Cleveland's Municipal Stadium mounted on moveable standards. If a hard-hitting club was coming to town, he would discreetly move the fences back. If the visiting team had weak hitters, he moved the fences in. Coincidentally, the Indians won the American League pennant in 1948. When Veeck's scheme was later revealed, the league passed a rule prohibiting changing the fence distances in mid-season.

6.17 **D. 60**

During the first part of the 1962 season, Mets owner Joan Whitney-Payson was out of the country. Before departing she asked that a daily telegram be sent to her to inform her of her team's progress. After receiving numerous messages detailing losses, she wired back: Please Tell Us Only When The Mets Win. "That was about the last word I heard from America," she recalled after her return. The 1962 Mets lost a modern-day record 120 games and gave up 948 runs, 322 more than any other NL team. They had losing streaks of nine, 11, 13 and 17 games and finished a whopping 60 games behind the first-place San Francisco Giants. The Mets were so bad they were loveable, and New Yorkers turned out in droves to watch their slapstick antics. Summing up the Mets' first-year performance, manager Casey Stengel noted: "The public that has survived one full season of this team has got to be congratulated."

I N   W H A T   Y E A R ?

In 1961, all attention focussed on the New York Yankees as Roger
Maris and Mickey Mantle staged their dual assault on Babe Ruth's
hallowed record of 60 homers in a season. It came to be known as the
year of the M&M Boys. Some baseball seasons are forever linked with
a slogan, a particular team or a major event. In this game, we ask you
to match the phrase to the year with which it is associated.

(Answers are on page 138)

| 1947 | 1948 | 1950 | 1951 | 1955 | 1956 |
| 1959 | 1960 | 1962 | 1964 | 1967 | 1968 |

1. "The Miracle at Fenway" _____

2. "The Go-Go Sox" _____

3. "The Shot Heard 'Round the World" _____

4. "The Whiz Kids" _____

5. "The Year of the Pitcher" _____

6. "Murtaugh's Men of Destiny" _____

7. "This Is Next Year" _____

8. "Spahn and Sain and Two Days of Rain" _____

9. "Don Larsen's Perfecto" _____

10. "The Amazin' Ones" _____

11. "The Great Experiment" _____

12. "The Philly Fade" _____

Chapter Seven

RECORD BREAKERS

They used to say that Lou Gehrig's streak of 2,130 consecutive games would never be broken. Now that Cal Ripken has demolished that one, it's time to find another candidate. How about Yogi Berra? At least three of his World Series records—most games (75), most at-bats (259) and most hits (71)—look safe for the ages. As long as the Series is played only once a year, it's hard to imagine any player appearing in 14 of them, as Berra did with the Yankees between 1947 and 1963. Now that we've dealt with that one, let's look at some other record-breaking performances from the glory years. *(Answers are on page 91)*

7.1   Which slugger topped his league in home runs a record seven consecutive years?

A. Hank Aaron
B. Willie Mays
C. Ralph Kiner
D. Mickey Mantle

7.2 **Which Yankee set a record by hitting safely in 17 straight World Series games?**
A. Mickey Mantle
B. Hank Bauer
C. Tony Kubek
D. Yogi Berra

7.3 **Who topped the AL in homers at age 20, making him the youngest player to ever win a league home run crown?**
A. Roy Sievers
B. Al Kaline
C. Tony Conigliaro
D. Willie Horton

7.4 **Who swatted a record-setting five grand slams in 1955?**
A. Al Rosen
B. Yogi Berra
C. Wally Post
D. Ernie Banks

7.5 **Who set a new standard for shortstops by driving in 149 runs in a single season?**
A. Vern Stephens
B. Lou Boudreau
C. Alvin Dark
D. Ernie Banks

7.6 **Which pitcher belted a record two grand slams in one game during the 1966 season?**
A. Don Drysdale
B. Earl Wilson
C. Tony Cloninger
D. Steve Blass

7.7 **Who hit homers in a record eight consecutive games in 1956?**
A. Charlie Maxwell
B. Gil Hodges

C. Dale Long
D. Joe Adcock

7.8 **Who is the only player to lead his league in eight different hitting categories in one season?**
A. Stan Musial
B. Frank Robinson
C. Ted Williams
D. Carl Yastrzemski

7.9 **Which American League pitcher set the major league mark for most strikeouts in a game, fanning 21 batters in a 16-inning game in 1962?**
A. Jim Bunning of the Tigers
B. Tom Cheney of the Senators
C. Camilo Pascual of the Twins
D. Dean Chance of the Angels

7.10 **Who struck out a record 17 batters in a World Series game?**
A. Carl Erskine
B. Sandy Koufax
C. Bob Gibson
D. Allie Reynolds

7.11 **Which hurler tossed a record-setting four no-hitters in four consecutive years?**
A. Sandy Koufax
B. Bob Gibson
C. Sam McDowell
D. Gaylord Perry

7.12 **Who fanned a record 181 batters in relief in 1964?**
A. Dick Radatz
B. Ron Perranoski
C. Al McBean
D. Hoyt Wilhelm

7.13 **Which outfielder handled a record 568 consecutive chances without an error from September 3, 1965, to June 4, 1967?**
A. Curt Flood
B. Paul Blair
C. Billy Williams
D. Vic Davalillo

7.14 **Which outfielder snagged a spot in the record books by making more than 500 putouts four times?**
A. Richie Ashburn
B. Jimmy Piersall
C. Willie Mays
D. Vada Pinson

7.15 **Which second baseman participated in a record-setting 161 double plays in 1966?**
A. Julian Javier
B. Glen Beckert
C. Joe Morgan
D. Bill Mazeroski

7.16 **Which team established an unwanted standard in 1966, when it was shut out 17 times?**
A. The Houston Astros
B. The Chicago Cubs
C. The Los Angeles Dodgers
D. The New York Yankees

Answers

RECORD BREAKERS

7.1 **C. Ralph Kiner**

Kiner's most famous utterance—"Home run hitters drive Cadillacs and singles hitters drive Fords"—underscored his special talent. Only Babe Ruth ever dominated the home run category the way Kiner did in his prime. His seven straight home run titles with the Pittsburgh Pirates, from 1946 to 1952, remains a major league record. If Kiner had played on a better team, his name would be better known today. The Bucs only escaped the second division once during the seven years that Kiner led the National League in homers, finishing in the cellar three times and twice in second-last.

7.2 **B. Hank Bauer**

Bauer hit safely in all seven games of the 1956 World Series against the Dodgers, in all seven games in 1957 versus the Milwaukee Braves, and in the first three games against the Braves in 1958, before Warren Spahn finally put an end to the streak, when he blanked the Yankees 3–0 on a two-hitter. During his 17-game streak, Bauer hit .316 with six homers and 16 RBI.

7.3 **C. Tony Conigliaro**

Conigliaro's career was curtailed by a serious beaning in 1967, leaving Boston Red Sox fans to wonder what might have been. Until then he had been hitting homers at a record pace for someone so young. Conigliaro hit 24 out of the park as a 19-year-old rookie in 1964, and followed that up by clubbing an American League-high 32 dingers in 1965, making him the youngest player to win a home run crown.

7.4 **D. Ernie Banks**

In 1955, the 24-year-old Texan suddenly emerged as dangerous slugger by cracking 44 homers. Five of Banks's blasts came with the bases juiced, setting a new major league mark for grand slams in a season. Jim Gentile of the Orioles tied the mark in 1961, but no one broke it until the Yankees' Don Mattingly clubbed six in 1987. Banks stroked 40 or more homers five times, a display of power that has not been matched by any other shortstop.

MOST HOMERS IN A SEASON BY A SHORTSTOP

Player	Team	Year	HR
Ernie Banks	Cubs	1958	47
Ernie Banks	Cubs	1959	45
Ernie Banks	Cubs	1955	44
Ernie Banks	Cubs	1957	43
Ernie Banks	Cubs	1960	41
Rico Petrocelli	Red Sox	1969	40
Vern Stephens	Red Sox	1939	39

7.5 **A. Vern Stephens**

A seven-time American League All-Star, Stephens enjoyed monster offensive seasons with the Boston Red Sox in 1948, 1949 and 1950. In 1949, he racked up 159 RBI to tie teammate Ted Williams for the league lead in the department and set a record for shortstops that has not been surpassed.

7.6 **C. Tony Cloninger**

Not only is Cloninger the only pitcher to hit two grand slams in a game, he is the only player in NL history to accomplish the feat. The Braves hurler delivered his two blasts versus the San Francisco Giants on July 3, 1966; the first one off pitcher Bob Priddy and the second off Ray Sadecki.

7.7 **C. Dale Long**

The six-foot-four, 205-pound first-sacker played 11 seasons in the minors before he finally won a full-time job at age 29 with the Pittsburgh Pirates in 1955. The next year, Long led the Bucs with 27 homers, smashing eight of them in a record eight consecutive games in May. (The record has since been equalled by Don Mattingly and Ken Griffey, Jr.). During that eight-game span, Long batted a sizzling .526 with 20 RBI.

7.8 A. Stan Musial

In 1948, Musial put together an extraordinary season, topping the National League in eight separate hitting categories: runs, hits, doubles, triples, RBI, total bases, batting average and slugging average. No other player has ever led in so many offensive departments. Musial's achievement has never gotten the attention it deserves because he did not break any records and he did not win the Triple Crown, falling one homer short. But for all-around excellence at the plate, it stands alone.

NL HITTING LEADERS (1948)

Category	Leader		Runner-Up	
Runs	Musial	135	Lockman	117
Hits	Musial	230	Holmes	190
Doubles	Musial	46	Ennis	40
Triples	Musial	18	Hopp	12
Home Runs	Kiner/Mize	40	Musial	39
Total Bases	Musial	429	Mize	316
Batting Ave.	Musial	.376	Ashburn	.333
Slugging Ave.	Musial	.702	Mize	.564

7.9 B. Tom Cheney of the Senators

On September 12, 1962, Cheney struck out a record 21 Baltimore Orioles in a 16-inning game. If not for this performance, Cheney, who compiled a career record of 19 wins and 29 losses, would be completely forgotten. As it is, his feat has never received much acclaim. Admittedly, it is not quite as impressive as Roger Clemens's mark of 20 strikeouts in a nine-inning game (which

Clemens has done twice), but Cheney deserves credit, not only for the 21 Ks, but for having the mettle to pitch a complete 16-inning game, which he won 2–1.

7.10   C. Bob Gibson

With the St. Louis Cardinals leading the Detroit Tigers 4–0 in the bottom of the ninth inning of game one of the 1968 World Series, pitcher Bob Gibson fanned Al Kaline. Seconds later, a roar went up from the crowd at Busch Stadium. Catcher Tim McCarver motioned to Gibson and started to walk towards the mound. Gibson, who liked to work quickly and hated being interrupted by visits from catchers, glowered at McCarver and yelled, "Give me the goddam ball!" But McCarver gestured again and finally Gibson turned and looked at the scoreboard, which was flashing a message that he had just equalled Sandy Koufax's Series record of 15 strikeouts in a game. The Cardinal pitcher touched his cap to acknowledge the fans, then screamed again at McCarver to give him the ball. Gibson then proceeded to fan Norm Cash and Willie Horton for his 16th and 17th strikeouts of the day, ending the game.

7.11   A. Sandy Koufax

Koufax tossed no-hitters in 1962, 1963, 1964 and 1965. The last one, versus the Chicago Cubs, was a perfect game. Koufax needed to be perfect to win the game. His mound opponent, Bob Hendley, allowed only one hit in the 1–0 defeat. The Dodgers pushed across their lone run when Lou Johnson walked, was bunted to second, stole third and scored on a wild throw by catcher Chris Krug.

7.12   A. Dick Radatz

There were few more intimidating sights for a hitter than watching six-foot-six, 230-pound Dick "the Monster" Radatz striding in from the bullpen. In three seasons with the Boston Red Sox from 1962 to 1964, the flamethrower fanned 487 batters in 414 innings. His high was 181 Ks in 1964, a record for relievers.

7.13   A. Curt Flood

Flood is best remembered today for challenging baseball's reserve clause, the first salvo in the players' fight for free agency. But during

Ernie Banks: Safe at home in a cloud of dust.

the 1960s, he was one of the best centre fielders in the game. In a year and half of baseball from 1965 to 1967, he handled the ball 568 times without making a single miscue.

7.14 A. Richie Ashburn

Was there ever a better defensive outfielder than Ashburn? It's tough to imagine who. There was no one more adept at running down fly balls. The Philadelphia Phillies centre fielder led the National League in putouts nine times in 10 years from 1949 to 1958. In four seasons Ashburn made more than 500 putouts. How rare is this? Only four other outfielders—Taylor Douthit, Chet Lemon, Dwayne Murphy and Dom DiMaggio—have made 500 putouts in a season, and none of them did it more than once.

NL OUTFIELD PUTOUT LEADERS (1949–1958)

Year	Player	PO	Runner-Up	PO
1949	R. Ashburn	514	B. Thomson	488
1950	R. Ashburn	405	B. Thomson	394
1951	R. Ashburn	538	D. Snider	382
1952	R. Ashburn	428	S. Jethroe	413
1953	R. Ashburn	496	G. Bell	447
1954	R. Ashburn	483	W. Mays	448
1955	B. Bruton	412	W. Mays	407
1956	R. Ashburn	503	W. Mays	415
1957	R. Ashburn	502	W. Mays	422
1958	R. Ashburn	495	W. Mays	429

7.15   D. Bill Mazeroski

Cubs shortstop Don Kessinger said about Mazeroski: "He was as good as I've ever seen at turning the double play. They called him "No Hands" because he threw so quickly he never seemed to touch the ball." Widely recognized as the best-fielding second baseman of all time, Mazeroski holds virtually all the career and season records for double plays. In 1966, he posted a sterling .992 fielding average, while taking part in an all-time record 161 twin killings.

7.16   C. The Los Angeles Dodgers

This is a peculiar record for a pennant winner to hold, but then the 1966 Dodgers didn't climb to the top of the National League on the strength of their batting. It was the club's superlative pitching staff, headed by 27-game winner Sandy Koufax, that led the way. The Dodgers were the second-lowest scoring team in the league in 1966 and they didn't have a single player reach 75 RBI. The Dodgers' lack of offense haunted them in the World Series, as the Baltimore Orioles swept the Californians in four games, holding them scoreless for 33 consecutive innings.

O D D   M A N   O U T

How sharp is your batting eye? In each of the 12 quartets listed
below, there is one name that does not belong. See if you can
spot the impostor. *(Answers are on page 139)*

1. Pitched a no-hitter:
   Juan Marichal, Whitey Ford, Hoyt Wilhelm, Warren Spahn.

2. Hit four homers in one game:
   Harmon Killebrew, Joe Adcock, Rocky Colavito, Gil Hodges.

3. Was voted Rookie of the Year:
   Pete Rose, Tony Kubek, Carl Yastrzemski, Orlando Cepeda.

4. Led the National League in ERA:
   Warren Spahn, Don Drysdale, Sam Jones, Phil Niekro.

5. Led the American League in home runs:
   Roy Sievers, Tony Conigliaro, Larry Doby, Al Kaline.

6. Won three games in a World Series:
   Harry Breechen, Sandy Koufax, Mickey Lolich, Lew Burdette.

7. Was a switch-hitter:
   Maury Wills, Nellie Fox, Red Schoendienst, Tom Tresh.

8. Hit a home run in first World Series at-bat:
   Roger Maris, Dusty Rhodes, Lou Brock, Brooks Robinson.

9. Played for the New York Mets:
   Yogi Berra, Warren Spahn, Duke Snider, Ron Santo.

10. Won a Cy Young award:
    Jim Kaat, Mike McCormick, Early Wynn, Vernon Law.

Chapter Eight

TRUE OR FALSE?

The Houston Astrodome originally had natural grass. True or False? It's funny how our memory plays tricks on us. The Astrodome was never supposed to have an artificial surface and it didn't have one during its first year of operation in 1965. The plastic turf became necessary because of a design flaw: the Dome's translucent roof panels diffused sunlight into a harsh glare that blinded outfielders. To solve the problem, the roof was painted with an acrylic coating. But that stopped sunlight from penetrating and killed all the grass. So, they installed the fake stuff in 1966.

(Answers are on page 102)

8.1   There is an asterisk affixed to Roger Maris's home run record. **True or False?**

8.2   Denny McLain was the era's only 30-game winner. **True or False?**

8.3   Fidel Castro once had a major league tryout? **True or False?**

8.4 Al Kaline was the youngest player in major league history to win a batting title. **True or False?**

8.5 Willie Mays never hit a home run in the World Series. **True or False?**

8.6 Mickey Mantle wore No. 7 throughout his career. **True or False?**

8.7 Sandy Koufax hit a home run in his first at-bat in the majors. **True or False?**

8.8 Mickey Mantle was the only player from the era to hit more than 40 homers in a season and post a batting average of higher than .350. **True or False?**

8.9 Jackie Robinson broke in with the Brooklyn Dodgers at second base in 1947. **True or False?**

8.10 Hank Aaron never hit 50 homers in a season. **True or False?**

8.11 Yogi Berra appeared as a player in all 15 World Series the New York Yankees were involved in between 1946 and 1968. **True or False?**

8.12 Luis Aparicio was known as "the Cuban Comet." **True or False?**

8.13 Lou Boudreau was the last player-manager to win a pennant. **True or False?**

8.14 Don Newcombe was the first black pitcher to win a game in the World Series. **True or False?**

8.15 Mickey Mantle is the only player to hit 50 or more homers and not lead his league in the category? **True or False?**

8.16 Whitey Ford lost more World Series games than any other pitcher. **True or False?**

8.17 Stan Musial, Ted Williams and Rocky Colavito all appeared in games as pitchers. **True or False?**

8.18 Ted Williams won his last batting title at age 40. **True or False?**

8.19 Felipe, Matty and Jesus Alou were the only trio of brothers to play in the majors during the era. **True or False?**

8.20 Roberto Clemente had more 200-hit seasons than any other player during the era. **True or False?**

8.21 Roberto Clemente was originally signed by the Brooklyn Dodgers. **True or False?**

8.22 Sandy Koufax was the only pitcher from the era to top his league in strikeouts four times. **True or False?**

8.23 Pete Rose was the first switch-hitter to win a National League batting title. **True or False?**

8.24 Jackie Robinson was never traded. **True or False?**

8.25 Robin Roberts was the only pitcher from the era to register 30 complete games in more than one season. **True or False?**

8.26 The award for the World Series MVP was first presented in 1955. No player from a losing team won the award through 1968. **True or False?**

Answers

T R U E O R F A L S E ?

8.1 False

Commissioner Ford Frick wanted some sort of distinctive mark placed beside Maris's single-season home run record to indicate he had achieved it in a 162-game schedule rather than in the 154-game schedule that Ruth played. But he never mentioned the word "asterisk" and no such mark exists in the record books.

8.2 True

When McLain posted 31 victories for the Tigers in 1968, it marked the first time since Dizzy Dean in 1934 that a pitcher had reached the 30-win plateau. Robin Roberts of the Phillies came the closest of any other pitcher in the era, when he registered 28 wins in 1952. No pitcher since has won 30 games.

8.3 True

History might have been very different if the Cuban dictator had a better curveball. Castro, who was a star pitcher at the University of Havana, flunked his tryout with the Washington Senators in 1947.

8.4 True

But just barely. When Kaline hit .340 in 1955 to win the AL batting crown at age 20, he was one day younger than Ty Cobb was when the Georgia Peach won his first batting crown in 1907.

8.5 True

Mays did not hit particularly well in any of the four World Series he appeared in, and he displayed little evidence of his formidable power. In 71 World Series at-bats, Mays batted .239 with 14 singles and three doubles, and no triples or homers.

8.6 **False**

Mantle wore No. 6 when he first joined the Yankees in 1951. Outfielder Cliff Mapes wore No. 7. It wasn't until after Mapes was traded to the St. Louis Browns on July 31, 1951, that Mantle inherited his trademark digit.

8.7 **False**

Far from hitting a homer, Koufax struck out in his first 12 at-bats in the majors in 1955. The Dodger mound ace never displayed much talent with the bat, posting an anemic .097 career batting average. It's scary to think what Koufax would have batted if he had been forced to hit against himself.

8.8 **False**

Only a handful of major leaguers have managed to hit 40 homers and bat .350 or more in a season. But Mantle, who hit .353 with 52 homers in 1956, wasn't the only player from the era to achieve the rare double. Norm Cash hit 41 homers and batted .361 for the Detroit Tigers in 1961.

8.9 **False**

Robinson played first base in his first year with the Dodgers. Eddie Stanky was the Dodgers' second baseman in 1947. When Stanky was traded in 1948, Robinson shifted to second base.

8.10 **True**

Aaron clubbed 40 or more homers eight times in his career, but he never once reached 50 in a season, which only makes his career total of 755 all the more remarkable.

8.11 **False**

Berra appeared as a player 14 times in the World Series between 1947 and 1963. However, when the Yankees met the Cardinals in the Fall Classic in 1964, the 39-year-old Berra was the Yankees' manager.

8.12 False

Aparicio was a Venezuelan. The Cuban Comet was the name applied to Aparicio's White Sox teammate, Minnie Minoso. The moniker perfectly captured Minoso's hustling playing style and zest for the game. Minoso led the AL in steals and triples three times, hit above .300 eight times and was a fan favourite everywhere he played.

8.13 True

Boudreau was a busy fellow in 1948. In addition to his managing duties with the Cleveland Indians, he played 151 games at shortstop and one game at catcher. He also batted .355 and copped the MVP award. Under Boudreau's leadership, the Indians captured the AL pennant and defeated the Boston Braves in the World Series.

8.14 False

In fact, Newcombe lost all four of his Series decisions. Brooklyn's Joe Black became the first black pitcher to win a game in the post-season, when he tossed a complete-game six-hitter to beat the Yankees 4–2 in game one of the 1952 Series.

8.15 False

When Mantle hammered 54 homers in 1961, only to finish second to Roger Maris and his total of 61, it marked the second time a player had hit 50 or more four-baggers and not led his league. The first to be similarily frustrated was Jimmie Foxx, who clubbed 50 homers for the Boston Red Sox in 1938, but placed second to Hank Greenberg of the Detroit Tigers and his league-leading 58 blasts. In 1996, a third player joined the list when Brady Anderson of the Baltimore Orioles hit 50 homers and placed second to Mark McGwire and his 52 dingers with the Oakland Athletics.

8.16 True

Ford owns the pitching marks for most losses and most wins in World Series competition. The Yankee great went 10–8 in 22 Series starts from 1950 to 1964. Ford also holds Series records for most games and most innings pitched, most strikeouts, most hits allowed and most bases on balls.

8.17 True

Musial, Williams and Colavito all took a turn on the hill during their careers. Musial tossed one perfect inning for the Cardinals in 1952. Williams worked two innings for the Red Sox in 1940, allowing three hits and one run. Colavito made two mound appearances, going three innings for the Indians in 1958 and two and two-thirds innings for the Yankees in 1968. He allowed no runs in his two pitching stints and posted a win in the second game.

8.18 True

No player has ever hit so well at an advanced age as Ted Williams, who won batting titles in 1957 and 1958, at ages 39 and 40.

THE OLDEST BATTING CHAMPIONS*

Player	Age	Year	Ave.
Ted Williams	40 years 1 month	1958	.328
Ted Williams	39 years 1 month	1957	.388
Honus Wagner	37 years 7 months	1911	.334
George Brett	37 years 4 months	1990	.329
Stan Musial	36 years 10 months	1957	.351
Luke Appling	36 years 5 months	1943	.328
Tony Gwynn	36 years 4 months	1996	.353

* CURRENT TO 1996

8.19 False

There were at least three other trios of brothers who played in the majors during the era. Clete and Ken Boyer had a third brother, Cloyd, who pitched five years in the bigs between 1949 and 1955; brothers Ed, Bob and Ted Sadowski all had brief stints in the majors in the 1960s; and the DiMaggio boys, Joe, Dom and Vince, were all still active in 1946.

8.20 False

Stan Musial had five 200-hit seasons during the era, one more than Clemente accumulated. Vada Pinson also had four.

8.21 **True**

The Dodgers signed Clemente for $10,000 in 1954, but the presence of Carl Furillo in right field left no room for the promising youngster, so he was sent to the Montreal Royals, the Dodgers' farm team in the International League. According to the rules of the day, any player signed for a bonus of more than $6,000 had to be put on a major league roster, otherwise they could be claimed by another team for $4,000. The Dodgers tried to hide Clemente by not playing him in Montreal, but the Pirates were not deceived. They claimed the future Hall of Famer on November 22, 1954.

8.22 **False**

Koufax's run of four strikeout titles in the 1960s was matched by Warren Spahn of the Braves, who led the NL in Ks in 1949, 1950, 1951 and 1952.

8.23 **True**

When Rose batted .335 to lead the National League in 1968, it marked the first time a switch-hitter had won a hitting crown in the senior circuit.

8.24 **False**

The 37-year-old Robinson was traded to the New York Giants on December 13, 1956, for pitcher Dick Littlefield and $30,000. However, the deal was cancelled when Robinson decided to retire.

8.25 **True**

Between 1946 and 1968, only three pitchers—Bob Feller, Juan Marichal and Robin Roberts—had seasons in which they pitched 30 complete games, and only Roberts managed the feat twice. The Phillies' workhorse registered 30 complete games in 1952 and went the distance 33 times in 1953.

8.26 **False**

Although the Yankees lost the 1960 World Series to the Pirates, New York's Bobby Richardson was voted MVP after he drove in a record 12 runs in the seven-game affair.

B U L L P E N   A C E S

Listed below are the first names of 17 of the era's top firemen. Find their last names in the puzzle by reading across, down or diagonally. Following our example of Elroy F-A-C-E, connect the other 16 names using the same letter no more than once. Start with the letters printed in heavy type.   *(Answers are on page 139)*

Elroy _____   Joe _____   Stu _____   Luis _____

Hoyt _____   Larry _____   Lindy _____   Clem _____

Ted _____   Phil _____   Frank _____   Jim _____

Ryne _____   Ellis _____   Ron _____   Turk _____

Dick _____

```
R  N  I  E  A  G  A  E
M  A  A  W  L  P  E  B  R  I
D  C  D  I  K  A  B  Y  N  K
A  T  H  L  O  L  I  H  A  S
L  Z  E  L  N  T  N  E  T  O
O  N  F  M  S  A  P  E  A  N
W  S  A—C  Y  N  L  R  R  R
D  R  H  E  T  O  Y  I  N  E
U  E  N  E  A  R  R  O  Z  L
R  E  N  K  R  R  Y  R  Y  L
   G  A  I  N  D  E  M  I
```

Chapter Nine

HEADLINE ACTS

I n 1954, Joe DiMaggio, who had been retired for three years, found a way to get back in the spotlight. He married the most famous blonde on earth: Marilyn Monroe. Gossip columnists dubbed the couple Mr. and Mrs. America. The marriage of the baseball god and the movie goddess lasted 274 stormy days. When the pair separated, sportswriter Oscar Levant noted: "It proves that no man can be a success at two national pastimes."

DiMaggio's marriage to Monroe was only one baseball-related story from the era that made the front page. In this chapter, we explore some other headline acts. *(Answers are on page 114)*

9.1 **Who flew 39 missions with the U.S. Marine Air Corps during the Korean War and survived a fiery crash in his F–9 fighter?**
A. Gil Hodges
B. Red Schoendienst
C. Ted Williams
D. Whitey Lockman

9.2 **Which event drew the largest crowd?**
A. "Babe Ruth Day" at Yankee Stadium in 1947
B. Satchel Paige's first major league start in 1948
C. Ted Williams's last game at Fenway Park in 1960
D. The New York Mets' home opener in 1962

9.3 **How much did it cost the Brooklyn Dodgers to acquire Jackie Robinson from the Kansas City Monarchs of the Negro Leagues?**
A. Nothing
B. $2,000
C. $5,000
D. $10,000

9.4 **In 1960, Cleveland Indians general manager Frank Lane announced: "I traded a hamburger for a steak." American League batting champion Harvey Kuenn was the steak. Who was the "hamburger" Lane sent to the Tigers in exchange?**
A. Norm Cash
B. Brooks Robinson
C. Rocky Colavito
D. Jim Bunning

9.5 **Which pitcher quit baseball in 1963 to become the youngest pro basketball coach in history, assuming the helm of the NBA's Detroit Pistons at age 24?**
A. Fred Lasher of the Twins
B. Aubrey Gatewood of the Angels
C. Jerry Casale of the Tigers
D. Dave DeBusschere of the White Sox

9.6 **Which member of the Philadelphia Phillies, pictured on the facing page, was gunned down by a deranged female fan during the 1949 season?**
A. Del Ennis
B. Mike Goliat
C. Jocko Thompson
D. Eddie Waitkus

A gunshot wound ended his season in 1949. Who is he?

9.7 **Which Boston Red Sox player went berserk and ended up in the violent ward of a mental institution in 1952?**
A. Hoot Evers
B. Jimmy Piersall
C. Mickey McDermott
D. Dom DiMaggio

9.8 **In 1953, Mickey Mantle walloped a 565-foot homer that many sources cite as "the longest, measured home run in a regular-season game." In what stadium did Mantle hit this titanic blast?**
A. Boston's Fenway Park
B. Washington's Griffith Stadium
C. Chicago's Comiskey Park
D. Kansas City's Municipal Stadium

9.9 **In 1966, Marvin Miller, the new head of the Major League Baseball Players' Association, convinced the owners to raise the minimum salary for players to what figure?**
A. $10,000
B. $20,000
C. $30,000
D. $40,000

9.10 **How did St. Louis Browns owner Bill Veeck make headlines in 1951?**
A. He installed an exploding scoreboard
B. He had his team outfitted in shorts
C. He staged a mock Martian invasion
D. He sent a midget up to bat

9.11 **In 1966, which pair of teammates staged the first dual-contract holdout in major league history?**
A. The Tigers' Al Kaline and Norm Cash
B. The Orioles' Jim Palmer and Dave McNally
C. The Dodgers' Sandy Koufax and Don Drysdale
D. The Pirates' Roberto Clemente and Willie Stargell

9.12 **On May 15, 1957, several Yankee players got into an altercation at a famous New York nightspot while celebrating Billy Martin's birthday. What was the name of the nightclub?**
A. The Playboy Club
B. Toots Shor's
C. The Copacabana
D. The Peppermint Lounge

9.13 **In 1965, Juan Marichal received an eight-game suspension and a $1,750 fine for attacking which catcher with his bat?**
A. Tim McCarver of the Cardinals
B. Joe Torre of the Braves
C. John Roseboro of the Dodgers
D. Chris Cannizzaro of the Mets

9.14 **Which manager was suspended for the entire 1947 season?**
A. Leo Durocher
B. Ben Chapman
C. Muddy Ruel
D. Billy Southworth

9.15 **What bizarre event occurred during a game at the Polo Grounds on July 4, 1950?**
A. A swarm of bees forced the cancellation of the game
B. A fan got into a fistfight with an umpire
C. A spectator was shot and killed
D. A plane crashed into the bullpen

9.16 **In 1959, Branch Rickey announced plans for the formation of a new major league baseball league. What was the league called?**
A. The American Association
B. The Continental League
C. The North American League
D. The National Baseball Confederation

9.17 **Who was novelist John Updike referring to when he wrote in 1960, "Gods do not answer letters"?**
A. Babe Ruth
B. Joe DiMaggio
C. Ted Williams
D. Stan Musial

Answers

HEADLINE ACTS

9.1 **C. Ted Williams**

Only a handful of ballplayers were inducted into the armed forces during the Korean War, and Williams, who was 33, married and a father, seemed an unlikely candidate. But because he had served as a flight instructor during World War II and had remained a member of the Marine Air Corps reserve, Williams was recalled into the service. He flew 39 combat missions over Korea, where one of his co-pilots was John Glenn, who later became the first American to orbit the earth. After 15 months overseas, the Splendid Splinter rejoined the Boston Red Sox in August 1953, and proceeded to hit an amazing .407 with 13 homers in 37 games.

9.2 **B. Satchel Paige's first major league start in 1948**

Although he was 42, and past his prime, Paige added another chapter to his legend when he joined Bill Veeck's Cleveland Indians midway through the 1948 season. On August 3, a crowd of 72,562 (a major league attendance record for a night game) turned out at Cleveland's Municipal Stadium to witness his first start, a 4–3 win against the Washington Senators. Paige set a Chicago attendance record of 51,013 in his next start, when he tossed a three-hit shutout versus the White Sox. But that was just the paid attendance. When informed of the sellout, thousands of frustrated fans stormed the gate and crashed into Comiskey Park, overwhelming the ticket-takers and uprooting turnstiles. By game time, the throng numbered more than 70,000. On August 20, 78,382 fans jammed into Municipal Stadium to watch Paige shut out the White Sox again, breaking the attendance mark he had

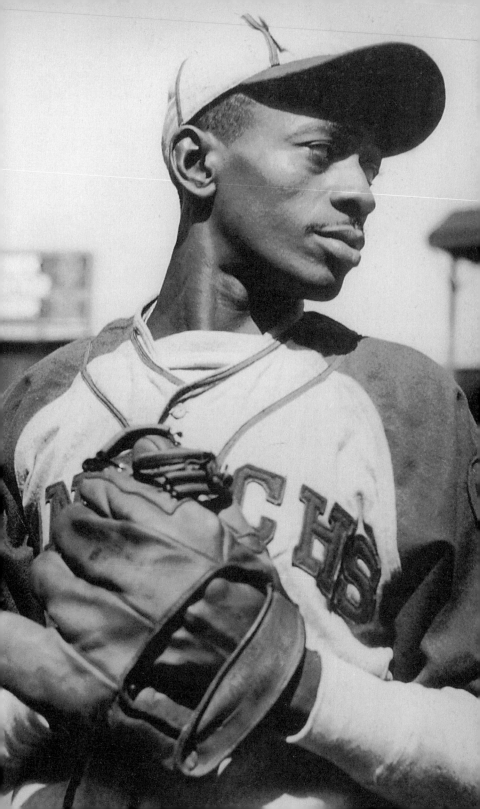

set 17 days earlier. In his first three starts, Paige drew more than 200,000 people. He finished the year with a 6–1 record and a 2.48 ERA and helped the Indians win the AL pennant, astounding baseball observers. Said Veeck: "Everybody kept telling me he was through. That was understandable. They thought he was human."

9.3 A. Nothing

Dodger president Branch Rickey received accolades for breaking the colour barrier by signing Jackie Robinson, but the method of the signing was classless. Rickey did not offer a cent in compensation to Tom Braid and J. L. Wilkinson, the owners of the Kansas City Monarchs, the team for which Robinson had played in the Negro Leagues. Nor did he pay any money when he snatched up 16 other Negro League stars for the Dodgers, including Roy Campanella, Don Newcombe and Junior Gilliam. Rickey justified his piracy by dismissing the Negro Leagues as fronts for racketeers and because they did not operate with standard player contracts. Said Rickey: "They are not leagues and have no right to expect organized baseball to respect them."

9.4 C. Rocky Colavito

Cleveland Indians general manager Frank "Trader" Lane loved to stir up controversy, but he topped himself when he sent fan favourite and American League home run king Rocky Colavito to the Detroit Tigers for batting champion Harvey Kuenn just before the opening day of the 1960 season. Irate Indians fans jammed the phone lines, ringing to express their displeasure. Lane's effigy was hung on lampposts. "Trader" Lane had become "Traitor" Lane. It didn't help matters when he told reporters, "What's the problem? All I did was trade a hamburger for a steak." The trade turned out badly for Lane. The hated Kuenn lasted only one season in Cleveland before he was dealt to San Francisco, while the Indians sank to the lower depths of the American League, where they would remain submerged for 35 years. Colavito had four banner seasons in Detroit, including a career year in 1961, when he clubbed 45 homers and 140 RBI. Said Tigers general manager Bill DeWitt: "I like hamburger."

9.5 **D. Dave DeBusschere of the White Sox**

The six-foot-six pitcher left the Chicago White Sox after two seasons to join the Detroit Pistons as a playing coach at age 24. DeBusschere played 10 seasons in the NBA, earning a reputation as a consummate team player and eventually gaining induction into the Basketball Hall of Fame. He later served as the commissioner of the American Basketball Association.

9.6 **D. Eddie Waitkus**

On June 14, 1949, at Chicago's Edgewater Beach Hotel, the Phillies first baseman responded to a cryptic message from a young woman named Ruth Ann Steinhagen, asking that he visit her room. Waitkus was no sooner inside when she pulled out a rifle and shot him in the chest. Steinhagen was arrested and booked for attempted murder, while Waitkus was rushed to hospital. The bullet had entered under his heart and lodged next to his spine, and doctors operated in a desperate bid to save his life. Though Steinhagen did not know Waitkus, she told police she had been in love with him for two years and had even built a shrine to him in her bedroom. His number was 36, so she bought records made in 1936. She started eating baked beans because he was born in Boston. When she discovered he was Lithuanian, she learned how to speak the language. Steinhagen was diagnosed as suffering from schizophrenia and was sent to a mental insititution. Amazingly, Waitkus not only survived, he returned to the majors the next season and helped lead the Phils to the World Series.

9.7 **B. Jimmy Piersall**

The 22-year-old rookie made a major splash with the Red Sox in 1952, not only with his dazzling glovework, but also with his outrageous antics. Piersall took elaborate bows after making catches, mimicked other players, screamed at umpires and flapped his arms like a seal. The bizarre behaviour was the prelude to a nervous breakdown which Piersall suffered later that year. He ended up in a mental hospital where he underwent shock therapy and counselling. Piersall eventually recovered and went on to play 17 years in the majors. His breakdown and return to baseball were detailed in the book, *Fear Strikes Out*, which was later made into a film.

9.8 **B. Washington's Griffith Stadium**

In a game against the Washington Senators on April 17, 1953, Mantle, batting righthanded, connected with a fastball delivered by southpaw Chuck Stobbs. The ball soared out of the park in left-centre at the 391-foot mark, caromed off a beer sign at the top of a 60-foot auxiliary scoreboard and disappeared over Fifth Street. Yankee publicity director Red Patterson promptly left the press box in pursuit of the ball. He found it in the hands of a 10-year-old boy named Donald Dunaway, who showed him where the ball had landed. Patterson then paced off the distance to the stadium's outfield wall. According to his calculations, the sphere had travelled an astonishing 565 feet. Patterson's account of tracking the ball down and measuring the distance it had covered captured the public's imagination, and the term "tape-measure job" suddenly entered baseball's lexicon.

9.9 **A. $10,000**

Although it sounds like a trifling sum by today's standards, Miller won a major concession from baseball's owners by getting them to raise the minimum player salary to $10,000 a season. That figure represented a $3,000 leap from the previous minimum of $7,000. In the 20 preceeding years, the minimum player salary had increased by only $5,000.

9.10 **D. He sent a midget up to bat**

Veeck was actually responsible for all the publicity stunts listed in the question, but the other three occurred when the maverick owner was running the Chicago White Sox. His most memorable prank with the Browns occured on August 19, 1951, during a doubleheader against the Detroit Tigers. The lead-off hitter for the Browns in the second game was supposed to be Frank Saucier. Instead Veeck sent up a pinch-hitter: three-foot-seven, 65-pound Eddie Gaedel. The tiny substitute's job was to simply crouch there with his bat on his shoulder and get a walk. To insure Gaedel did not get any bright ideas, Veeck told him that a rifleman on the stadium roof would have him in his sights and would squeeze the trigger if he dared swing. Pitcher Bob Cain, who was laughing too hard to get the ball over the plate, walked Gaedel on four pitches.

Then, a pinch-runner took over. It was Gaedel's last appearance as a player. American League president Will Harridge promptly banned the use of midgets, describing their participation as "conduct detrimental to baseball."

9.11 **C. The Dodgers' Sandy Koufax and Don Drysdale**
Before the start of the 1996 season, Sandy Koufax and Don Drysdale staged an unprecedented joint holdout, demanding that the Dodgers pay them a half-million dollars each over three years; a considerable hike from the $70,000 they had both earned the year before. They also demanded that the Dodgers negotiate with them through Koufax's lawyer, J. William Hayes. In the end, the two Dodger aces did not get exactly what they had asked for. They had to settle for one-year deals and Hayes was frozen out of the negotiations. Still, the Dodgers did agree to pay Koufax $120,000 and Drysdale $105,000 for the 1966 season, which made them the two highest-paid pitchers in the game.

9.12 **C. The Copacabana**
On May 15, 1957, Mickey Mantle, Billy Martin, Hank Bauer, Whitey Ford, Yogi Berra and Johnny Kucks, along with a few of their wives, arrived at the Copacabana to celebrate Martin's 29th birthday and catch a performance by Sammy Davis, Jr. Their party soon got into an argument with a bowling team from the Bronx that was shouting racial obscenities at Davis. One of the hecklers, Edwin Jones, a 200-pound delicatessen owner, invited Bauer to settle the dispute with his fists. In the resulting melee, someone flattened Jones, fracturing his jaw and giving him a concussion. The scuffle got a lot of play in the New York papers and though the Yankee players insisted it was a Copa bouncer who had coldcocked Jones, they were all fined. Yankee general manager George Weiss used the incident as pretext to trade Martin, whom he viewed as a negative influence on Mantle, to Kansas City.

9.13 **C. John Roseboro of the Dodgers**
The combination of a hot pennant race, a hot day and a hot rivalry combined to produce a boiling controversy when the Giants and Dodgers met on August 22, 1965, at Candlestick Park. In the early

innings, both starting pitchers, Sandy Koufax and Juan Marichal, threw brushback pitches, but things really got ugly in the third when Marichal came up to bat for the first time. After Koufax's third pitch, Marichal suddenly turned and clubbed catcher John Roseboro in the head, opening a two-inch gash and igniting a full-scale brawl. Marichal claimed he was provoked by Roseboro, who, in returning Koufax's pitch, had fired the ball back so close to his head it actually nicked his ear. NL president Warren Giles fined the Giants' ace $1,750 and suspended him for eight games. Roseboro filed a $110,000 battery suit against Marichal. Four years later, he settled out of court for $7,500.

9.14   A. Leo Durocher

In April 1947, baseball commissioner Happy Chandler suspended Durocher for the season. No specific reason was given. Chandler cited conduct "detrimental to baseball." Durocher was already in hot water with the baseball establishment due to his friendship with several gangsters, including Bugsy Siegel, but the incident that prompted his suspension involved Larry MacPhail, the general manager of the New York Yankees and a close friend of Chandler. Durocher, who had already been reprimanded by Chandler for consorting with gamblers, spotted MacPhail sitting with two notorious gamblers at an exhibition game in Havana in 1947 and spouted off to columnist Dick Young about this apparent double standard. When Young quoted Durocher in his column, MacPhail went ballistic and pressured Chandler to take action against the Dodger skipper, which he did. Everyone was shocked by the severity of the punishment. "Leo is like the fellow who passed a red traffic light and got the electric chair," wrote Arthur Daley in the *New York Times*.

9.15   C. A spectator was shot and killed

On July 4, 1950, 56-year-old Bernard Doyle was one of 50,000 fans gathered at the Polo Grounds to view a Dodgers-Giants double-header. Doyle had just turned to speak to a fan sitting next to him when he suddenly slumped forward with blood pouring from his left temple, and died. Doyle had been struck by a bullet. The story made the front page. Despite a criminal investigation it was never determined where the shot came from, but police suspected it had been fired from outside the stadium.

9.16   B. The Continental League

Convinced that the major leagues were not keeping up with the westward population shift, Rickey announced plans to form a new baseball league, with teams in such untapped markets as Atlanta, Houston, Dallas, Denver, Minneapolis, Toronto and Montreal, as well as in New York, to fill the void left by the departed Dodgers and Giants. The league never became a reality as major league owners moved to grant new franchises to carefully targeted cities before Rickey's organization could be launched. Still, Rickey, the man who revolutionized baseball by signing Jackie Robinson, had once again transformed the sport by pushing the majors into expansion.

9.17   C. Ted Williams

The famous line appeared in a *New Yorker* magazine piece entitled "Hub Fans Bid Kid Adieu," in which Updike recounts Williams's last game in a Red Sox uniform, on a cold and blustery day at Fenway Park in September 1960. The tempermental star had feuded with fans and the Boston press corps throughout his career and the residue of the quarrel could be observed after his last at-bat in the big leagues, when, in storybook fashion, he belted a home run. Head down and unsmiling, Williams quickly circled the bases and vanished into the dugout. Ignoring the crowd's applause and the "We want Ted" chants, Williams stayed put. Updike wrote: "The papers said that the other players, and even the umpires on the field, begged him to come out and acknowledge us in some way, but he never had and did not now. Gods do not answer letters."

T H E   B E S T   B A T S

Although batting average is baseball's best-known hitting statistic, it's a limited tool in evaluating a hitter's overall prowess. The problem with batting average is that it gives equal value to a single as it does a home run, and it ignores bases on balls, which are as important an offensive factor as singles. In an effort to supply a more accurate picture of a batter's ability, stats gurus such as Pete Palmer and Bill James have come up with various mathematical formulas for rating hitters. The drawback of these systems is their complexity. The average fan can't follow the calculations, and so the numbers, interesting as they may be, carry little weight.

A simpler method is to combine a player's on-base percentage and his slugging average. To calculate on-base percentage, you add up a player's hits, walks and hit by pitches, and divide the total by his at-bats, walks and hit by pitches. To calculate slugging average, you add up a player's total bases (a single counts as one base, a double as two bases and so on) and divide the sum by his at-bats.

A superior on-base percentage is anything above .400. A superior slugging average is anything above .600. Combine the two and you have a good gauge of a batter's ability to get on base and hit for power, which is what the art is all about.

Using this stat—let's call it offensive production (OP)—here are the top 10 single-season performances from the glory years.

OFFENSIVE PRODUCTION (1946-68)

Year	Player	OBP	SA	OP
1957	Ted Williams	.528	.731	1.259
1957	Mickey Mantle	.515	.665	1.180
1956	Mickey Mantle	.467	.705	1.172
1946	Ted Williams	.497	.667	1.164
1948	Stan Musial	.450	.702	1.152

1961	Norm Cash	.488	.662	1.150
1949	Ted Williams	.490	.650	1.140
1961	Mickey Mantle	.452	.687	1.139
1947	Ted Williams	.499	.634	1.133
1948	Ted Williams	.497	.615	1.112

Clearly, the era's best performances belong to Williams and Mantle. The lone National Leaguer to crack the list is Musial. The one anomaly is Cash, who never came close to the 1.000 OP level in any other season in his career.

Babe Ruth posted the best single-season OP total in history in 1920. He had an on-base percentage of .530 and a slugging average of .847, for an amazing score of 1.377. In fact, Ruth owns six of the eight best single-season OP tallies of all-time. The other two belong to Ted Williams, whose performances in 1941 and 1957 rank fourth and fifth on the chart. Not surprisingly, Ruth and Williams rank one-two in career OP totals.

CAREER OFFENSIVE PRODUCTION

Player	OBP	SA	OP
Babe Ruth	.474	.690	1.164
Ted Williams	.483	.634	1.117
Lou Gehrig	.447	.632	1.079
Jimmy Foxx	.428	.609	1.037
Hank Greenberg	.412	.605	1.017
Rogers Hornsby	.434	.577	1.011
Mickey Mantle	.423	.557	.980
Joe DiMaggio	.398	.579	.977
Stan Musial	.418	.559	.977
Johnny Mize	.397	.562	.959

Chapter Ten

THE FALL CLASSIC

"**P**itching is 75 per cent of baseball," said Connie Mack. That's never more true than in the Fall Classic. The dominant role played by pitchers is evident in the voting for the World Series MVP. From 1955, the year it was first presented, until 1968, pitchers won the award 12 times. Of the 12 hurlers who won MVPs, only one failed to post more than one victory in a Series. Can you guess his identity? The answer is obvious if you think perfection.

In this last chapter, we embark on a chronological cruise through the glory years, recalling some of the highs and lows of baseball in October.

(Answers are on page 130)

10.1 **Which Cardinal scored the winning run against Boston in the 1946 Series, racing home from first on Harry Walker's hit?**
A. Stan Musial
B. Marty Marion
C. Enos Slaughter
D. Whitey Kurowski

10.2 Don Larsen tossed the only World Series no-hitter in 1956, but another Yankee hurler came close in game four of the 1947 Series. Who lost his bid for immortality when Brooklyn's Cookie Lavagetto doubled with two outs in the bottom of the ninth?
A. Vic Raschi
B. Bill Bevens
C. Spud Chandler
D. Allie Reynolds

10.3 Which rookie won the playoff game that clinched the 1948 pennant for the Cleveland Indians, pitched a shutout against the Boston Braves in game three of the Series, then came out of the bullpen to save the decisive sixth game?
A. Satchel Paige
B. Mike Garcia
C. Steve Gromek
D. Gene Bearden

10.4 Although the Yankees defeated the Dodgers in the 1952 tilt, Brooklyn's Duke Snider established a new NL post-season record. What did Snider do?
A. He hit six doubles
B. He hit four homers
C. He drove in 12 runs
D. He rapped five hits in one game

10.5 The Yankees won their fifth straight world championship in 1953, downing the Dodgers in six games. Which pinstriper provided the offensive fireworks, hitting .500 and driving in eight runs?
A. Mickey Mantle
B. Hank Bauer
C. Billy Martin
D. Yogi Berra

10.6 Willie Mays's sensational running catch of a long drive in the 1954 World Series remains one of the most dramatic moments in baseball history. Which Cleveland Indians player hit the ball that dropped into Mays's mitt?

A. Jim Hegan

B. Vic Wertz

C. Al Rosen

D. Bobby Avila

10.7 After losing five straight World Series to the Yankees, the Brooklyn Dodgers finally defeated their crosstown rivals in 1955. Who blanked the Yanks in game seven to clinch Brooklyn's first world championship?

A. Johnny Podres

B. Carl Erskine

C. Roger Craig

D. Don Newcombe

10.8 Which ex-Yankee led the Milwaukee Braves to glory in 1957, posting three complete-game Series wins, including two shutouts, against his former team?

A. Don McMahon

B. Johnny Sain

C. Warren Spahn

D. Lew Burdette

10.9 Which pitcher was the toast of Los Angeles after he posted two wins and two saves to spark the Dodgers to victory over the Chicago White Sox in the 1959 Series?

A. Danny McDevitt

B. Larry Sherry

C. Stan Williams

D. Clem Labine

10.10 In 1960, the Pittsburgh Pirates upset the New York Yankees, capturing game seven on Bill Mazeroski's homer in the bottom of the ninth. What else was noteworthy about the 1960 Series?

A. Mazeroski's homer was the only one hit by the Pirates

B. All four Pirates' wins came on their last at-bat

C. Mickey Mantle hit for the cycle in game six

D. The Yankees scored more runs than any team in Series history

10.11 In the 1961 Series, an ankle injury forced Whitey Ford to leave game four in the sixth inning, but not before he had set a new record for consecutive shutout innings pitched in Series play. The mark had belonged to which former Yankee?

A. Allie Reynolds

B. Lefty Gomez

C. Babe Ruth

D. Red Ruffing

10.12 Who snared Willie McCovey's line drive in the bottom of the ninth inning, with two on and two out, to preserve the Yankees' 1–0 victory in game seven of the 1962 Series?

A. Tony Kubek

B. Roger Maris

C. Bobby Richardson

D. Moose Skowron

10.13 Who set a Series record by rapping 13 hits in the 1964 duel between the St. Louis Cardinals and the New York Yankees?

A. Lou Brock

B. Ken Boyer

C. Bobby Richardson

D. Mickey Mantle

10.14 After dropping the first two games of the 1965 Series, the Los Angeles Dodgers rallied to defeat the Minnesota Twins in seven games. Sandy Koufax won two games and Don Drysdale one, but it was the other unsung member of the Dodgers' "big three" who won the pivotal fifth game, on a five-hit shutout. Who was he?

A. Ed Roebuck

B. Bob Miller

C. Claude Osteen

D. Johnny Podres

10.15 The Dodgers set a record for futility in the 1966 Series by failing to score a run in how many consecutive innings against the Baltimore Orioles?

A. 18

B. 23

C. 28

D. 33

10.16 Which hurler registered a one-hitter in the 1967 clash between the St. Louis Cardinals and the Boston Red Sox?

A. Jim Lonborg

B. Jose Santiago

C. Bob Gibson

D. Nelson Briles

10.17 Although St. Louis lost the 1968 Series to Detroit, Cardinals pitcher Bob Gibson set a new Series mark for strikeouts. How many hitters did he fan in his three starts?

A. 27

B. 31

C. 35

D. 39

Answers

THE FALL CLASSIC

10.1 C. Enos Slaughter

Earlier in the 1946 Series, Slaughter had been held up at third by coach Mike Gonzalez on a play on which Slaughter felt he could have scored. He complained so much that Cards manager Eddie Dyer told him, "If it happens again and you think you can score, go ahead. I'll take the rap." Slaughter did just that in the bottom of the eighth inning of game seven, sprinting home from first on Harry Walker's weak liner to left-centre and easily beating shortstop Johnny Pesky's relay throw to the plate. The run broke a 3–3 deadlock and put the Cards ahead to stay.

10.2 B. Bill Bevens

The only World Series start of Bevens's career was a memorable one. Battling control problems, he had given up eight walks in the game, and two of them, plus a sacrifice and an infield out, had cost him a run in the fifth inning. Still, entering the ninth, the Yankees led 2–1 and Bevens's no-hitter was still intact. With one out, Carl Furillo walked. Spider Jorgensen then fouled out. Al Gionfriddo ran for Furillo and stole second. Yankee manager Bucky Harris ordered Bevens to intentionally walk Pete Reiser. Eddie Miksis ran for Reiser and Cookie Lavagetto pinch-hit for Eddie Stanky. On Bevens's second pitch, Lavagetto lashed a double off the right-field wall breaking Bevens's no-hitter and driving in both runners to win the game for the Dodgers. Ironically, the three key players in the drama—Bevens, Lavagetto and Gionfriddo—never played another year in the majors.

10.3 D. Gene Bearden

The outstanding pitcher on the 1948 Indians' staff was not Bob
Feller or Bob Lemon, but rather 27-year-old rookie Gene Bearden,
who used a dancing knuckleball to post a 20–7 record and an AL-
leading 2.43 ERA. Bearden beat the Boston Red Sox in a one-game
playoff to seal the pennant for the Indians and then bedeviled
another Boston team, the NL Braves, with his knuckler in the World
Series. With the Series knotted at one game apiece, Bearden shut
down the Braves on a five-hitter in game three, then came out of
the bullpen to squelch a Braves rally in the Series' decisive sixth
encounter. The magic Bearden had working for him in 1948 mys-
teriously vanished after the Series. He never won more than eight
games in a season again.

10.4 B. He hit four homers

Prior to 1952, no National Leaguer had ever hit more than two
homers in the Fall Classic. The Duke of Flatbush broke the mark
in game six and then connected again later in the same game to join
Babe Ruth and Lou Gehrig as the only players to belt the ball over
the fence four times in one Series. The stage was set for Snider to
break the mark in dramatic fashion when he came to bat in the seventh inning of game seven, with the Dodgers trailing 4–2 and the
bases full. But Yankee reliever Bob Kuzava got him to pop out.
Amazingly, Snider repeated the feat by stroking four homers
against the Yankees in the 1955 Series, this time in a winning cause.
Though Reggie Jackson now owns the record for most homers in a
Series with five, Snider is still the only player to go deep four times
in more than one Series.

10.5 C. Billy Martin

The 1953 Series featured two powerhouse offenses. The New York
Yankee lineup included Mickey Mantle, Yogi Berra, Hank Bauer
and Gene Woodling. The Brooklyn Dodgers had Duke Snider,
Jackie Robinson, Roy Campanella and Gil Hodges. Yet when the
dust had cleared, the man of the hour was the weakest hitter on
either club—Yankee second baseman Billy Martin. A .257 hitter
during the regular season, Billy the Kid went wild, batting .500

with 12 hits (both records for a six-game Series), including two homers and eight runs batted in. Martin's bases-loaded triple sparked the Yanks to a 9–5 win in game one, and it was his clutch single off Clem Labine in the bottom of the ninth inning of game six that drove in the Series-winning run.

10.6   B. Vic Wertz

If not for Mays's sensational catch, the first game of the 1954 Series would be remembered as Vic Wertz's shining moment. In his first three at-bats of the Series lidlifter, the Cleveland first baseman had two singles and a triple and had driven in both of his team's runs. The score was tied 2–2 when Wertz came to bat in the eighth inning with two runners on base. Wertz connected off reliever Don Liddle, sending a towering drive to dead centre. Mays raced to the wall and, with his back to the plate, snared the fly directly in front of the 460-foot sign. Against any other outfielder the ball would have fallen in for a triple, driving in both runners and giving Wertz four RBI on the day. As it was, the Indians failed to score in the inning and the Giants eventually won the game in the 10th on a three-run pinch-hit homer by Dusty Rhodes. The Indians never recovered from the opening-game setback, succumbing in four straight.

10.7   A. Johnny Podres

Although he only posted a 9–10 record during the 1955 season, Podres proved to be the answer to Dodger prayers in the World Series. The young lefty was the only pitcher on Brooklyn's staff to go the distance against the Yankees as the Dodgers won their first World Championship. Podres tossed a complete-game seven-hitter to win game three at Ebbets Field on his 23rd birthday, then came back in game seven to humble the Bronx Bombers in their own backyard on an eight-hit shutout.

10.8   D. Lew Burdette

Burdette, who appeared in two games for the Yankees as a rookie in 1950, was dealt to the Braves in 1951. The trade came back to haunt New York in the 1957 Series when Burdette blanked the Yankees for 24 consecutive innings. His scoreless string began in the fourth inning of game two, which Burdette won 4–2. He stifled the Bronx Bombers in game five, outduelling Whitey Ford to win 1–0. Then, pitching on just two days' rest, Burdette went the distance in game seven to shut out New York again, 5–0, to give Milwaukee its first world championship.

10.9 B. Larry Sherry

In 1959, for the first time in Series history, no complete games were pitched by a member of either staff. Not surprisingly then, it was a relief pitcher who stole the show. Larry Sherry, a 24-year-old rookie, played a pivotal role in all four Dodger victories against the Pale Hose, picking up two wins and two saves and fashioning a 0.71 ERA in 12 ⅔ innings of work.

10.10 D. The Yankees scored more runs than any team in Series history

New York's offense shattered numerous records in the 1960 Series, batting .338 as a club, scoring 55 runs and collecting 91 hits and 27 extra-base blows, as the Yankees overwhelmed the Pirates in their three wins by scores of 16–3, 10–0 and 12–0. Even though the Bucs hit just .256 as a team and their pitching staff posted a horrendous 7.11 ERA, they came out on top where it mattered most—in the win column.

1960 WORLD SERIES TOTALS

	W	R	H	2B	3B	HR	RBI	AVE	BB	SO	ERA
Pittsburgh	4	27	60	11	0	4	26	.256	12	26	7.11
New York	3	55	91	13	4	10	54	.338	18	40	3.54

10.11 C. Babe Ruth

The year 1961 was not a vintage one for the Babe. Roger Maris broke his single-season home run record and then in the Series Whitey Ford broke another of Ruth's cherished records—the mark for most consecutive scoreless innings by a pitcher. Though he never took the mound for the Yankees in a Series game, Ruth put together a streak of 29 ⅔ scoreless innings in his two trips to the Series with the Boston Red Sox in 1916 and 1918. Ford surpassed the record by running his shutout skein to 32 innings against the Cincinnati Reds in 1961. Ford's string of 33 ⅔ scoreless innings was snapped in the second frame of the first game of the 1962 Series by the San Francisco Giants.

10.12 C. Bobby Richardson

The Yankees led the Giants 1–0 in the bottom of the ninth of the 1962 Series with two outs and runners on second and third, when Willie McCovey strode to the plate to face pitcher Ralph Terry. Yankee manager Ralph Houk called time and came out to talk to Terry. First base was open and conventional wisdom dictated that the Yankees should intentionally walk the lefthanded slugger and opt to pitch to righthanded-hitting Orlando Cepeda. But Terry wanted to take his chances with McCovey and Houk gave in. On Terry's third pitch, McCovey hit a screaming liner towards right. But second baseman Bobby Richardson threw up his glove and snagged the ball to give the Yankees another world championship. The memory of the moment stayed with McCovey a long time. In 1986, when he was inducted into the Hall of Fame, a reporter asked him how he would like to be remembered. Said McCovey: "I'd like to be remembered as the guy who hit that line drive over Bobby Richardson's head to win the 1962 World Series."

10.13 C. Bobby Richardson

Tim McCarver and Ken Boyer were the hitting stars for the St. Louis Cardinals as they edged the New York Yankees in seven games in the 1964 Series, but it was Bobby Richardson who batted a sizzling .406 for the losers and set a new post-season record with 13 hits.

10.14 C. Claude Osteen

After beating Dodger aces Don Drysdale and Sandy Koufax in the first two games of the 1965 showdown, the Minnesota Twins looked ready to take a stranglehold on the Series in game three. But lefty Claude Osteen stymied the Twins on a five-hit shutout to give the Dodgers some breathing room and the National Leaguers rallied to win the Series in seven.

10.15 D. 33

The Los Angeles Dodgers scored only twice against the Baltimore Orioles in the 1966 Series, one run coming on a homer by Jim Lefebvre in the second inning of the first game and the other on a bases-loaded walk in the third frame of the same game. After that, the Dodgers put up nothing but zeroes for the next 33 innings of the Series, going down in four straight games. In their ineptitude, the Dodgers set new Series marks for fewest runs scored (2), fewest hits (17) and lowest batting average (.142).

10.16 A. Jim Lonborg

The 1967 Series might have had a different result if the Boston Red Sox had not been forced to use Lonborg in the last game of the season in order to clinch the American League pennant. To give him an extra day of rest, the Red Sox started their Cy Young winner in game two, missing a matchup with the Cardinals' Bob Gibson in the opener. Lonborg dazzled the Cards in his first two starts, winning game two, 5–0, on a one-hit shutout and tossing a three-hitter to win game five, 3–1. But when he was forced to go head-to-head against Gibson in game seven on only two days' rest, Lonborg did not have his customary zing and he was routed by the Cardinals, who won the decisive encounter, 7–2.

10.17 C. 35

Gibson struck out 17 Detroit Tiger batters in game one of the 1968 Series, then fanned 10 in game four and eight in game seven for a record total of 35. In doing so, he eclipsed his own mark for most strikeouts in a Series, set in 1964, when he fanned 31. However, the record was small consolation for the ferociously competitive Gibson, who lost game seven 4–1 in a tense pitching duel with Mickey Lolich, ending his streak of seven consecutive complete-game Series wins. As it turned out, it was Gibson's last appearance in a World Series.

Game Answers

GAME 1: WILLIE, MICKEY & THE DUKE

1. **Willie Mays** was voted Rookie of the Year in 1951.
2. **Duke Snider** hit four homers in the 1952 and 1955 World Series.
3. **Mickey Mantle** won MVP awards in 1956, 1957 and 1962.
4. **Willie Mays** topped the 100-RBI mark 10 times in his career.
5. **Duke Snider** hit 40-plus homers five straight years from 1953 to 1957.
6. **Willie Mays** won 12 Gold Glove awards.
7. **Mickey Mantle** won a Triple Crown in 1956.
8. **Willie Mays** stole 40 bases in 1956.
9. **Willie Mays** hit four homers in one game in 1961.
10. **Duke Snider** spent his entire career in the outfield. (Mays and Mantle played other positions at various times.)
11. **Mickey Mantle** led the AL in runs scored six times.
12. **Willie Mays** hit homers in three All-Star games.

GAME 2: BY ANY OTHER NAME

PART I	PART II
1. L. Orlando Cepeda	1. G. Edwin Snider
2. A. Whitey Ford	2. J. Lawrence Berra
3. J. Harmon Killebrew	3. H. Albert Schoendienst
4. H. Bob Turley	4. F. John Powell
5. B. Frank Howard	5. A. Harold Reese
6. D. Ken Harrelson	6. C. Fred Walker
7. I. Harvey Haddix	7. B. William Skowron
8. E. Willie McCovey	8. L. Charles Stengel
9. C. Brooks Robinson	9. E. Forrest Burgess
10. K. Al Rosen	10. D. Leroy Paige
11. F. Vernon Law	11. I. James Rhodes
12. G. Phil Rizzuto	12. K. George Tebbetts

GAME 3: INFIELD CHATTER

1. Willie Mays
2. Hank Aaron
3. Stan Musial
4. Brooks Robinson
5. Sandy Koufax
6. Warren Spahn
7. Boog Powell
8. Bob Gibson
9. Joe DiMaggio
10. Gaylord Perry
11. Don Drysdale
12. Ted Williams
13. Mickey Mantle
14. Satchel Paige
15. Pete Rose
16. Yogi Berra

GAME 4: STRIKE 'EM OUT

| OLIVA | RUNNELS | FAIN, MAYS | ASHBURN |
| FURILLO | KALINE | DAVIS | MANTLE |

They all won league batting crowns.

GAME 5: ALL-STAR NUMBERS

NATIONAL LEAGUE		AMERICAN LEAGUE	
Left field: Hank Aaron	44	Left field: Ted Williams	9
Centre field: Willie Mays	24	Centre field: Mickey Mantle	7
Right field: Roberto Clemente	21	Right field: Frank Robinson	20
Third base: Eddie Mathews	41	Third base: Brooks Robinson	5
Shortstop: Ernie Banks	14	Shortstop: Luis Aparicio	11
Second base: Bill Mazeroski	9	Second base: Nellie Fox	2
First base: Stan Musial	6	First base: Harmon Killebrew	3
Catcher: Roy Campanella	39	Catcher: Yogi Berra	8
Pitcher: Sandy Koufax	32	Pitcher: Whitey Ford	16

GAME 6: IN WHAT YEAR?

1. "The Miracle at Fenway" — 1967
2. "The Go-Go Sox" — 1959
3. "The Shot Heard 'Round the World" — 1951
4. "The Whiz Kids" — 1950
5. "The Year of the Pitcher" — 1968
6. "Murtaugh's Men of Destiny" — 1960

7. "This Is Next Year"—1955
8. "Spahn and Sain and Two Days of Rain"—1948
9. "Don Larsen's Perfecto"—1956
10. "The Amazin' Ones"—1962
11. "The Great Experiment"—1947
12. "The Philly Fade"—1964

GAME 7: ODD MAN OUT

1. Whitey Ford
2. Harmon Killebrew
3. Carl Yastrzemski
4. Don Drysdale
5. Al Kaline

6. Sandy Koufax
7. Nellie Fox
8. Lou Brock
9. Ron Santo
10. Jim Kaat

GAME 8: BULLPEN ACES

Elroy Face
Hoyt Wilhelm
Ted Abernathy
Ryne Duren
Dick Radatz

Joe Page
Larry Sherry
Phil Regan
Ellis Kinder

Stu Miller
Lindy McDaniel
Frank Linzy
Ron Perranoski

Luis Arroyo
Clem Labine
Jim Konstanty
Turk Lown

ACKNOWLEDGEMENTS

The author gratefully acknowledges the help of W. C. Burdick
of the National Baseball Hall of Fame, Jocelyn Clapp and Norman
Currie of UPI/Corbis-Bettmann, Joanna Bruno of AP/World
Wide Photos, editor Brian Scrivener, designer Peter Cocking,
Rob Sanders and Terri Wershler of Greystone Books and the
many baseball writers whose brilliant prose has helped to
illuminate the game.

PHOTO CREDITS

ABOUT THE AUTHOR

Kerry Banks is an award-winning journalist and sports columnist.
He is also the co-author of *Ultimate Hockey Trivia*.